CHRISTMAS FOR THE *Heart*

25 Devotions Reclaiming the Beauty and Wonder of the Season

Christmas for the Heart

Cheryl Barker

B&H Publishing®
Brentwood, Tennessee

Printed in China

979-8-3845-0855-7

Published by B&H Publishing Group
Brentwood, Tennessee

Published in association with the literary agency
of Credo Communications, LLC, Grand Rapids,
Michigan, credocommunications.net.

Dewey Decimal Classification: 242.33
Subject Heading: DEVOTIONAL LITERATURE /
CHRISTMAS / JESUS CHRIST—NATIVITY

Cover design by Jonathan Lewis; Jonlin Creative.
Cover images by Kerry Norgard/Arcangel and siripornt/
shutterstock. Author photo by Kim Jones Photography.

1 2 3 4 5 • 28 27 26 25

For my grandsons Isaiah, James,
Samuel, and Silas.
May you draw ever closer to
Jesus at Christmas and always.

CONTENTS

PREFACE

Christmas stirs all kinds of longings in our hearts. We long for a joyful and peaceful celebration of the season. We yearn for merry moments with those we love, for nostalgic moments filled with sweet memories, and also for meaningful moments of worship. Simply put, we long for the beauty and wonder of Christmas.

But so much tries to get in the way of that kind of Christmas celebration. Pressure-packed schedules, the desire and drive to do everything Christmas, disillusionment with the commercialism of the season, and discouraging life situations can all hinder our Christmas longings from becoming reality.

I want to help change that for you. With this book, I hope to help you reclaim the beauty and wonder of Christmas. What better gift could I give?

In fact, Christmas has been a time for gifts ever since that momentous, life-changing night in ancient Bethlehem, when God gave the world the gift of a Savior, when baby Jesus took his first breaths and began drawing people to himself. Mary and Joseph were the first to gaze on this greatest gift from God. The shepherds then came, drawn like a magnet to the manger where the baby Jesus—the King of kings and Lord of lords—first shined his light in our world. Later on, in response to this greatest gift from God, the Magi came from the East to worship the Babe and offer him gifts fit for a king. And with that, many say our tradition of gift-giving at Christmas was born.

It has been my great joy and privilege for nearly all my adult life to continue to shine the light of Jesus during the holiday season by including an original poem in my Christmas cards. I consider each one a little gift for the heart to all my family and friends, written with the help of the Author of Christmas himself.

You'll find many of those poems in the following pages, along with reflections, quotes, Scriptures, holiday activities, and guided journaling opportunities. All designed to help you reclaim the beauty and wonder of Christmas. All designed to help you fully celebrate the season, to rejoice in the greatest gift ever given to the world, and to inspire you to give the King of kings the worship he's due.

And so, my friends, I give you *Christmas for the Heart: 25 Devotions Reclaiming the Beauty and Wonder of the Season.* And I give it to you with the love of Christ. May he draw you like a magnet to himself this holiday season!

1

WELCOME, BEAUTIFUL CHRISTMAS

"Be merry all, be merry all,
With holly dress the festive hall,
Prepare the song, the feast, the ball,
To welcome merry Christmas."[1]

WILLIAM SPENCER

THANKSGIVING HAS COME AND GONE, and the early days of a new Christmas season stand at the doorway of our hearts, awaiting an eager welcome. If you listen closely, even now you may imagine hearing a knock at the door, like a happy announcement that it's time, that the days to prepare for Christmas are here. If you listen with the ears of your spirit and soul, you may even hear a voice—the King of Christmas himself—calling you to begin your celebration. Reminding you to rejoice in him.

Yes, Christmas carries with it an air of excitement, the warmth of home and family, all treasured things touched by tradition, and the joy of Christmas worship. Childhood memories bubble to the surface, bringing out the kid in all of us as we recall the thrill of holiday activities on magical December nights. Or we remember the love and laughter of our family gathered in the living room while watching favorite Christmas movies. And we mustn't forget the years of playing the role of a bleating sheep or an angel with a crooked halo in the Christmas pageant at church.

Warm memories like these from our early days help us welcome the season each year. Charles Dickens said, "It is good to be children sometimes, and never better than at Christmas, when its mighty Founder was a child himself."[2] Just like children, the anticipation of Christmas can also make our grown-up hearts smile. That's especially true when we're trying to create similar heartwarming memories for our own children or grandchildren.

Sometimes, though, if we're honest, a feeling of panic or some other negative emotion may try to intrude on the merry moods our hearts yearn to feel or pass on to others. Too much to do, too little time, expectations, normal daily demands, and unexpected interruptions or disappointments of life try to steal our joy. It's happened to me time and again over the years.

Let's not let any Christmas-spirit thieves worm their way into our hearts this year. Instead, let's take a few simple steps to alleviate the pressures where possible.

We can postpone appointments or tasks that aren't absolutely necessary, plan for super simple meals, cut back or simplify gift-giving in some way, and forgo activities or traditions that drain us rather than give us joy. Let's each take the steps needed in our own lives to reduce our stress and then determine to celebrate and enjoy the season with joyful abandon.

Join me, won't you? The magic and merry, the holly and holy await. Let's reclaim and welcome a beautiful Christmas!

Beautiful Christmas

Beautiful Christmas, I welcome you,
Come in and dwell with me,
Deck my home with joy and laughter
String love lights on the Christmas tree.

Beautiful Christmas, please go with me
Give cheer to those I greet,
Warm hearts with simple acts of kindness
Look closely for the unseen need.

Beautiful Christmas, shine everywhere
Touch all with peace and goodwill,
Bring light to even the darkest corners
Grant hope, speak "Peace, be still."

Beautiful Christmas, I know you now
The Bethlehem Babe you are,
I welcome you, come dwell with me,
Lead me by the light of your star.

*"On that day the Branch of the LORD
will be beautiful and glorious."*

Isaiah 4:2

Christmas WISDOM

Determine to celebrate and enjoy the season with joyful abandon, making the adjustments needed to do just that.

Christmas PRAYER

Jesus, I long to fully welcome this season of celebrating your birth. Please help me

Christmas PAST

One of my favorite ways of welcoming Christmas when I was growing up was

Christmas PRESENT

I am welcoming Christmas this year by

Christmas MERRYMAKING

Hold your own little Christmas welcoming ceremony. String lights around your front door or light a Christmas candle—or any number of other symbolic holiday activities—and sing "Joy to the World" or "O Come, All Ye Faithful." As you create a Christmas ambiance in your home, you'll set the stage for Christmas worship in your heart.

2

THE LIGHT OF CHRISTMAS

"O Father, may that Holy star
Grow every year more bright,
And send its glorious beams afar
To fill the world with light."[3]

WILLIAM CULLEN BRYANT

AS DECEMBER'S EARLIEST HOURS PEEK over the holiday horizon with a faint glow of the days to come, our yearning for the Christmas season to be filled with magic and light is birthed once again. At the same time, the unspoken hope that the season itself will brighten our lives, whatever our current circumstances, makes its annual debut as well. We long to set aside our cares and enjoy a fairy-tale Christmas, one that offers every heartwarming touch possible. But if we look just beneath that surface longing, we'll see a deeper longing for abiding joy and everlasting light for our souls.

Often we manage to manufacture or stumble upon some of that surface holiday magic and light—scenes from a fairy-tale Christmas. But even then, the merry feelings are often short-lived. Real life intrudes like clockwork, like the monthly bills that arrive without fail. Like the last day of summer vacation.

Yes, kids who whoop and holler with glee over their gifts and play in noisy harmony will soon commence quarreling, ending up in tears while still clutching their new toys. The harmony has now evaporated. A couple returns home one evening, still shining with the glow from a lovely holiday outing, and steps into a growing puddle as the kitchen floor floods from a leaking pipe under the sink. Their contented smiles drop like those of two kids finding coal in their Christmas stockings. And even more common, many of us—after experiencing a splendid Christmas—find our holiday joy melting away after everyone goes home and we return to everyday life with its everyday challenges. Our temporarily forgotten struggles have surfaced again. We come face-to-face once more with our real need, our need for true light and life.

I'm reminded of the passage in God's Word known as the love chapter. "If I speak human or angelic tongues but do not have love, I am a noisy gong or a clanging cymbal. If I have the gift of prophecy and understand all mysteries and all knowledge, and if I have all faith so that I can move mountains but do not have love, I am nothing. And if I give away all my possessions, and if I give over my body in order to boast but do not have love, I gain nothing" (1 Cor. 13:1–3).

The same kind of discerning insight can be applied where our deepest Christmas longing is concerned. If we have a home filled with twinkling lights, gaily wrapped gifts, the merry strains of holiday classics, and our loved ones laughing nearby but do not have in our hearts the adoration and worship of Jesus, the true light of Christmas, we have nothing lasting. Nothing that will satisfy our soul's deepest longing. Nothing that will never fail us.

Today and during each holiday season, may we renew our focus on that perfect and everlasting Light who burst upon the world scene centuries ago and has been shining an unparalleled light for us ever since. In the New Testament, Matthew 4:16 quotes from the prophet Isaiah and says, "'The people who live in darkness have seen a great light, and for those living in the land of the shadow of death, a light has dawned.'" Oh, how I thank God for that great Light!

So remember with me, won't you, that no magic, no joys, no light the world can offer will fill the deepest yearning of our hearts. Only Jesus, the true Light of Christmas. Only Jesus, the Savior of the world. May we let the wonder we seek be found in him. May we let him satisfy our longing hearts.

The Light of Christmas

What's that on the horizon,
The light of Christmas drawing near?
Possibly the promise of a miracle,
Maybe the drying of a tear?

Near and far people look
For the light of Christmas to be theirs,
Yearning for the hope it holds
Longing to cast aside their cares.

Some seek the light in merrymaking
Others in the warmth of home,
Some think that things can offer comfort
Some choose the world to roam.

But the light of Christmas that satisfies,
The hope that will never let us down,
Is the miracle found in a manger—
The Christ Child born in Bethlehem town.

"I am the light of the world. Anyone who follows me will never walk in the darkness but will have the light of life."

John 8:12

Christmas **WISDOM**

For lasting joy and eternal light, fix your eyes on the Christ child, the Light of the world, this Christmas.

Christmas **PRAYER**

Jesus, be my light this Christmas and beyond as I

Christmas **PAST**

My favorite memories of holiday lights and the joy they bring include

Christmas PRESENT

This Christmas I will try to point others to the true Light of Christmas by

Christmas MERRYMAKING

Grab some friends or family members and enjoy a new Christmas light experience this season. Find a light display you've never seen, go on a candlelight tour you've not yet experienced, or attend a tree-lighting ceremony or candlelight church service you've not attended before. Enjoy some new-to-you Christmas lights with loved ones this year!

3

THE CHRISTMAS STORY

"Look back reverently across the centuries to the stable in Bethlehem . . . Hear the cry of a tiny infant . . . hear the distant strains of singing angels."[4]

JONI EARECKSON TADA

STORIES ARE POWERFUL. THEY CAPTURE our attention. And if told effectively, they keep our attention. Stories entertain us or enlighten us or both. They help us remember information and ideas. Stories have the power to stir emotion and empathy. They connect us and can ultimately change us.

During the Christmas season, we are surrounded by reminders of one of the most powerful stories of all time—of the night Jesus was born. Manger scenes can be seen adorning the yards of many churches, homes, or even businesses. Star decorations light the top of countless Christmas trees, and ornaments inspired by the Christmas story grace their branches. Christmas pageants and living nativity productions draw crowds without fail each year as they remind people of a story God orchestrated more than two thousand years ago.

This story of Christmas captured attention from the moment an angel of the Lord burst through the night sky and announced it to ordinary shepherds who were keeping watch over their flock in a field near Bethlehem. As the glory of the Lord shone around the shepherds, this messenger of God held them captivated. Immediately after he delivered his lifesaving, world-changing announcement, the miraculous-meter went up another notch when an entire host of angels joined him in lifting praises to God. The shepherds' attention could never waver with a story like that breaking out around them.

This amazing story straight from heaven not only captured their attention, but it enlightened the shepherds as well. The biggest and best news they could have ever heard rang in their ears. The long-awaited Messiah, the Savior of the world, had been born!

But the angel didn't stop with that—he gave details. This infant Savior, Christ the Lord, had been born that very day in Bethlehem. The shepherds would find him wrapped in swaddling clothes. And lying in a manger of all things. Furthermore, the angel told them this good news was for all people. So yes, this story enlightened the shepherds, and they would never forget the message they heard, the story they witnessed. It would be forever etched in their memories.

Consider, too, the emotions the shepherds must have felt as this magnificent story fell on their ears. They surely experienced everything from fear to awestruck amazement, to joy and peace and giddy excitement as they ran to find the baby Jesus. And when they saw him? We can only imagine the wonder, the joy, the reverence, the humble worship the Christ child inspired in them.

What about the connections and changes this story wrought? Just think about it. Heaven connected with earth—the very God of the universe with the people he created—first through his heavenly messengers and then through Jesus himself. The infant Savior's very presence drew the shepherds to him, where they also met Mary and Joseph, and then shared the good news with any who would listen. Yes, connections were made. And were the shepherds changed? I venture to say they were never the same again. Were others who heard the good news changed? Undoubtedly.

Let's never lose sight of the beauty, wonder, and power of this miraculous story, this tale of our Savior's birth. It's still capturing and keeping attention today. It's still enlightening us and helping us remember that God sent Jesus to save us, to make us his children forever. It's still stirring emotion. It's still connecting us. And yes, praise God, still changing us. We'll never be the same again. Ever.

The Story of Christmas

The story of Christmas began long ago
With ordinary people like us,
When God chose Mary to bear his Son
And in Joseph placed his trust.

As Mary's time of delivery drew near
A journey they had to make
To Bethlehem, a town unaware,
Of the glory they would soon partake.

No room for them could be found
Except a stable so forlorn,
But what better place could e're there be
For the Lamb of God to be born?

This precious Son, this Lamb of God,
Became the sacrifice for our sin,
And now we all can be forgiven
And have eternal life with him.

This is the reason we celebrate,
This is the reason we sing,
Our Christmas is merry because of him—
Have you made him your Savior and King?

"This is how the birth of Jesus the Messiah came about."

Matthew 1:18 NIV

Christmas WISDOM

Let the Christmas story capture your attention in a variety of ways and change your life this holiday season.

Christmas PRAYER

Lord, when I think of the story of your birth and how you came to be our Savior, I

Christmas PAST

One of my earliest memories of hearing the Christmas story happened

Christmas **PRESENT**

I will make the Christmas story an important part of my celebration this year by

Christmas **MERRYMAKING**

Make the telling of the Christmas story a family affair during your Christmas celebration this year. Gather everyone together and hand out the various figures from your nativity set. As you or one of the other adults tell the story, have each family member place his or her figure near the manger when that character is mentioned. The story will come to life, capturing and keeping the attention of all. I first saw this idea in action as my brother-in-law Keith told the story to our family years ago. Tradition-worthy for sure.

4

A CROWDED CHRISTMAS

"We expect too much at Christmas. It's got to be magical. It's got to go right. Feasting. Fun. The perfect present. All that anticipation. Take it easy. Love's the thing. The rest is tinsel."[5]

PAM BROWN, AUSTRALIAN POET

IT HITS ME ALMOST EVERY year as Christmas draws near. Life suddenly overwhelms and panic rises. It might be triggered by something as simple as the flip of the calendar to December, or perhaps an unexpected demand or an unforeseen problem becomes the tipping point. I'm guessing you've experienced this too.

Maybe a loved one has emergency surgery and requires extra care upon returning home. Maybe you yourself end up in bed for several days with the flu and remain weak as a kitten for another week. Whatever the reason, the question "How will I ever be able to get everything done?" comes rushing through, threatening to squeeze out all hope for Christmas joy and peace as the holiday freight train gathers steam.

It's easy to understand why such panic intrudes each year during the holidays. We love the season—the traditions, the tasty food, the special activities. We want to do it all. Even when we realize we need to simplify, we find it hard to bring ourselves to part with any aspect of the season. I've struggled with this myself. What will I give up? Sending out my Christmas cards? Making my favorite Christmas goodies? Gift-giving? No, those things are too important to me.

But within all our efforts to do everything, one thing is missing: peace. We're so busy trying to keep the panic at bay while doing our crowded Christmas, we miss the peace the angels spoke of as they praised God in that field near Bethlehem so many years ago.

Think of Mary with her newborn baby on that first Christmas night. She, too, must have felt a bit of panic once the shepherds started spreading the news about Jesus. Scripture tells us: "When they had seen him, they spread the word concerning what had been told them about this child, and all who heard it were amazed at what the shepherds said to them" (Luke 2:17–18 NIV). How quickly do you suppose people started lining up to see the little one the shepherds were calling the Savior of the world, as the angels had referred to him? Anxiety could easily have gripped Mary with concerns for the baby's health and safety, her own exhaustion, or the lack of suitable surroundings to host visitors.

Instead, in the midst of this swirl of events, emotions, and people, Mary took time to pull away—if only in her thoughts—to store up for safekeeping the memories of everything happening to them. Luke 2:19 tells us: "But Mary was treasuring up all these things in her heart and meditating on them." She took time to think about the unfolding of the story and to consider the meaning and wonder of it all. She took time for herself. For God. For peace.

What do we need to do to reclaim the beauty and wonder of the peace God longs to give us during the Christmas season? What changes do we need to make? What can we trim from our schedules and our holiday must-do lists to free up more time for the things that are truly important—things like personal worship, peace, and more of the simple joys at the heart of the season?

If we can't bring ourselves to let go of any of our beloved Christmas traditions and activities, maybe we can simplify them in some way. For example, we could still decorate our homes but not with as many decorations as usual. Or we could buy gifts for a family stocking for each family represented, rather than filling individual stockings for everyone. And if we can't bear to change our treasured traditions at all, then other adjustments to our schedules and obligations become imperative. Otherwise, we'll lose all hope of avoiding a Christmas crowded with too many demands on our time and energy.

Whatever strategy we choose for simplifying, let's do it early and let's do it faithfully. Even as you go through this book, please don't feel pressured to add every "Christmas Merrymaking" activity to your lives. They are just ideas for you to consider implementing to enrich your Christmas celebration. Maybe you'll just try one or two each season. Whatever works for you.

Bottom line? Be flexible, make adjustments, and choose wisely. Each and every Christmas, let's say *no* to crowded days and yes to peace.

A Crowded Christmas

None of us long for a crowded Christmas
One where peace cannot be found,
None of us dream of frenzied days
Where push and pull abound.

If pull we must, let's pull back,
Our jam-packed holiday let's trim,
Let's make room for what's important
No more filling to the brim.

Time for family and traditions
Time for friendship and for rest,
Time to reach out, time to worship,
Time to bless and be blessed.

The only crowded Christmas we need
Is one crowded with simple things,
So let's fill the season with joy, with love,
And with the peace the Christ Child brings.

"Peace I leave with you.
My peace I give to you."

John 14:27

Christmas WISDOM

Saying no to certain things allows you to say yes to the best things—at Christmas and all year long.

Christmas PRAYER

Lord, help me focus on peace, joy, and love this Christmas by

Christmas PAST

One simple holiday tradition that brought me great joy in the past was

Christmas PRESENT

I will simplify my holiday season this year by

Christmas MERRYMAKING

After dinner one evening, serve up some ice cream—holiday style! Offer peppermint, French eggnog, or gingerbread ice cream while discussing simplifying strategies with your loved ones. In the process, you'll discover which Christmas traditions and activities are most important to them and which ones you can forgo. Gain practical help while merrymaking. A win-win for everyone.

5

THE MARVELOUS MIX OF CHRISTMAS

"I do hope your Christmas has had a little touch of Eternity in among the rush and pitter patter and all. It always seems such a mixing of this world and the next—but after all, that is the idea!"[6]

EVELYN UNDERHILL

Aah, Christmas! Such a fun yet meaningful holiday. The perfect mix of magic and miracles. Just think about it. Everything changes as December draws near.

Our eyes may notice the changes first. Familiar surroundings magically morph from run-of-the-mill to merry—from our homes, neighborhoods, and shopping districts to our places of work, worship, and play. Whether marked by earthly traditions or touches of heaven, all begin to sparkle and shine with the joy and thrill of the season. Colorful Christmas trees and twinkling lights, Santas and snowmen, wreaths and reindeer, worshipful nativities and peaceful candlelight all tell the world a celebration has commenced. Christmas is here. Joy to the world!

Soon our ears detect the magic and miracles as well. Strains of favorites like "White Christmas," "Santa Claus Is Coming to Town," and "Winter Wonderland" set our minds awhirl with all the fun and excitement Christmas brings. But then the beloved carols of the season pull our focus back to the miracle that's responsible for our celebration in the first place. And all the while, we hear the jingle of bells, shoppers humming to piped-in holiday music, and voices calling out, "Merry Christmas!" All remind us that wherever we turn, the most wonderful time of the year surrounds us.

Next, distinctive fragrances add to the mix of this special season. Not only do they please our senses, but they also stir up some of our oldest and most cherished memories. Whether cider simmering on the stove or holiday candles working their magic, the classic scents of Christmas put smiles on our faces and contentment in our hearts. We need only bring in a tree fresh cut from a farm and bake our favorite Christmas cookies to complete our perfect mix of Yuletide aromas. Soon the miracle of nostalgia comes to full bloom. Memories so real we can practically taste and touch them wrap us in their tender embrace and we are transported back. Back to the best of our holiday histories. Magic and miracles, indeed.

Add to the miraculous taste of memories the life-giving taste of God's Word through the reading of the Christmas story. And then, of course, the taste of everything else Christmas envelops us too. That's when the holiday mix takes on a new magic. Not long after we catch the first whiff of our Christmas baking, we'll soon be sampling a bite of our favorite cut-out cookies or tasty seasonal breads. The results of our annual candy-making will also delight our taste buds along with the savory treats and holiday drinks we indulge in year after year. After all, Christmas isn't Christmas without our favorite traditional fare passing our lips.

The Christmas mix is completed by touch but encompasses far more than what our bodies may feel. Yes, the chill of December nips at our noses, the toasty warmth of crackling logs in the fireplace brings comfort, and the hugs of loved ones along with touches shared as we reach out to others make our hearts happy. But deeper comfort and contentment fill our souls as we add the spiritual aspects of the season to our Christmas mix. We look across the centuries and remember how God reached down to touch the world with his amazing love through the birth of his perfect Son. When we respond in worship by reaching back to him, his healing touch of love, forgiveness, and eternal hope changes everything. The miracle of Christmas is ours.

So much wonder, so much beauty to reclaim in this most wonderful time of the year, isn't there? Let's do it. Let's reclaim the perfect Christmas mix.

The Marvelous Mix of Christmas

Christmas is a marvelous mix
A medley of tradition and faith,
A beautiful blend of heaven and earth,
A merry and holy holiday.

A marvelous mix of magic,
Of music in the air,
Of snowflakes, angels, and twinkling lights
Of sweet surprises shared.

A marvelous mix of memories
From childhood through present day,
Starring friends and family dear
Ever in our hearts they'll stay.

A marvelous mix of ministry
Of reaching out to others,
Giving and serving with goodwill to all,
All become sisters and brothers.

Christmas—a marvelous mix of miracles
Begun by a Babe and his star,
Still ripples down through the ages
Bringing Light and Life from afar.

*"How great are his miracles,
and how mighty his wonders!"*

Daniel 4:3

Christmas WISDOM

Allow yourself to enjoy both the magic and the miracles that embody the Christmas season.

Christmas PRAYER

Lord, as I consider the Christmas mix that would please you, would you help me balance

Christmas PAST

Snapshot memories that most clearly capture the marvelous mix of my past Christmases include

Christmas PRESENT

I want my life to reflect the marvelous mix of Christmas this year by

Christmas MERRYMAKING

Take time one evening or throughout the season to read holiday-themed stories or books that reflect both the magic and miracles of Christmas. Balance books like Frosty the Snowman *and* The Night Before Christmas *with ones like* A Charlie Brown Christmas *and* The Best Christmas Pageant Ever. *Read out loud to someone else or even by yourself. Either way will be a blessing!*

6

CONNECTING THROUGH CHRISTMAS GREETINGS

"Many merry Christmases, many happy new years, unbroken friendships, great accumulation of cheerful recollections, affections on earth, and heaven at last, for us all."[7]

CHARLES DICKENS

MERRY CHRISTMAS, EVERYONE! 'TIS THE season for greetings. Written as well as spoken.

Sending and receiving "Merry Christmas" wishes clearly numbers among the manifold joys of the season. The heart-warming and festive nature of the holidays inspires us to connect with people near and far, friends old and new. No wonder Christmas is known as the most wonderful time of the year. Reaching out, however briefly, and connecting to those who have touched our lives in some way is one reason why.

The mode for sending Christmas greetings has changed for many over the past several years, ever since digital photography ushered in new ways of doing a number of things. For some the traditional Christmas card or letter has given way to a family-photo card complete with holiday design and a tailor-made message. And due to the rising costs of postage, many people have stopped mailing Christmas greetings altogether. A portion of them may email their greetings now while many others post holiday family photos on social media. Whatever the means during the Yuletide season, people love connecting with and hearing from one another. That most certainly has not changed.

As for me, count me among those who are keeping the old-fashioned card-in-the-mail tradition alive—though I do enjoy sharing family photos on social media as well. As far as Christmas cards go, though, I delight in blessing others with beautiful cards that open to include a brief personal message as well as an original Christmas poem each year. I also love that this allows me to play a merry part in maintaining the age-old tradition of sending season's greetings in the mail. John Greenleaf Whittier said, "For somehow, not only at Christmas, but all the long year through, the joy that you give to others is the joy that comes back to you."[8] Indeed, it gives me joy to send joy to others through my Christmas cards. It gives me joy to share the words God has given me for my poem each year. It gives me joy to connect.

During the holidays, not only do we all seem to have this almost innate desire to connect and communicate with those who hold special places in our hearts, many of us also feel a yearning to connect with the Lord—the One who holds all of us in his hands.

This goes back to the very first Christmas. Just think about Simeon, a hope-filled character on the fringes of that amazing story of Jesus's birth. He saw his dream of connecting with the Messiah come true when Mary and Joseph took Jesus to the temple forty days after his birth to present him to the Lord. Simeon, whom Scripture describes as "righteous and devout" (Luke 2:25), was awaiting the Messiah and the comfort he would bring to the people of Israel. The Holy Spirit had even revealed to Simeon that he would not die before he saw Christ. Just imagine the joy he must have felt when he finally laid his longing eyes on Jesus and held him in his arms. Ah, the sweetness of that particular connection with the Divine!

Though none of us today will ever go through quite the same experience with the Lord that Simeon did, we still understand and experience the yearning to connect with him in a special way, especially at Christmastime.

For those of us who've already given our hearts to the Creator of the universe, he is our Father, our Savior, our Friend. Our hearts swell with gratitude, love, and praise at the magnitude of what he did for us on that holy night in ancient Bethlehem, on the night when Jesus was born as Immanuel—God with us. It seems only natural to respond to this miracle of love with our love and worship in return, only natural to long to connect with him during these special days as we remember and celebrate his birth. For those who are not yet believers, any who place their faith in Jesus will one day also want to draw close and commune with him.

So, my friends, in your desire to connect with the Lord this season, imagine this: If you could send a Christmas card or letter to God today, what would it say? What do you long to tell him? How would your heart overflow?

Go ahead. Say it. And send it with love.

A Christmas Letter to God

Dear Lord, Christmas finds us sending greetings
To loved ones far and near,
Cards and letters filled with warmth
And wishes for the coming year.

This year I long to send this letter
Overflowing with thanks and love
To you, my God, my Lord, my Savior,
My King and Counselor from above.

My message this Christmas is simple, Lord,
As I think of you coming to earth,
Coming to live among us,
Bringing new life, giving new birth.

My heart and my pen cry out today,
"Thank you, Father, for sending,
Thank you, Jesus, for coming,
Thank you, Spirit, for staying!"

With love,
Cheryl

"'The virgin will conceive and give birth to a son, and they will call him Immanuel' (which means 'God with us')."

Matthew 1:23 NIV

Christmas WISDOM

Take advantage of the tradition of sending Christmas greetings, connecting and sharing your love and life with others near and far.

Christmas PRAYER

Father, when I think of that first Christmas when you sent Jesus to be our Savior, I long to tell you

Christmas PAST

My most precious memories of receiving special Christmas cards or letters include

Christmas PRESENT

I will send Christmas greetings this year by

Christmas MERRYMAKING

Gather your immediate family and make a short video wishing other family members and friends a "Merry Christmas." Have fun putting your family's personality into it. Make it funny, nostalgic, musical, or whatever other approach best suits your crew. When it's ready to go, text it to whomever you want. This will be more personal than posting it on social media. Plus, your loved ones will easily be able to view the video again when they want to see your smiling faces and hear your sweet voices. Keep your traditional mode of sending Christmas greetings if you'd like, but add this idea to the mix in some way. Your loved ones will be glad you did!

7

THE PERFECT CHRISTMAS GIFT

"What can I give Him, poor as I am?
If I were a shepherd, I would bring a lamb;
If I were a Wise Man, I would do my part;
Yet what I can I give Him: give my heart."[9]

CHRISTINA ROSSETTI

WE'VE ALL EXPERIENCED IT. THAT deep desire to give the perfect Christmas gift to someone we dearly love or want to bless. Our hearts can literally ache with the need. Oh, how we long to give our loved one or friend the special joy of being known inside and out—of being completely understood.

My earliest memories of longing to find the perfect Christmas gifts revolve around my parents. I so wanted them to be pleased when they opened the presents I gave them on Christmas morning. Of course, my first attempt at perfect gifts reflected my young age. On the day Mom took my sisters and me to our local five-and-dime to do our Christmas shopping, I automatically made a beeline for the candy aisle. Wow, talk about a Christmas wonderland. I soon walked out of there thrilled with my find: two chocolate-covered marshmallow Santas wrapped in brightly colored foil with Santa's image right on the front.

I knew I'd found the perfect gifts for Mom and Dad. And I was right. With beaming faces and sparkling eyes, they oohed and aahed over their marvelous presents.

As I got a little older, my efforts at giving my parents the perfect Christmas gifts grew slightly more sophisticated. Well, at least less sugary. I graduated to cute little animal figurines for Mom's shadowbox and socks for Dad. And if their reactions were any indication, I'd still managed to give them the perfect gifts.

Decades have gone by now and as a mother and a grandmother, I still long to give my loved ones the perfect Christmas gifts. Oh, how I want the presents I give them to bring them joy. It's doubly satisfying if I can land on something that's especially meaningful to them for some reason.

I have to admit, though, that even with loving desires motivating me, I've too often fallen into the trap of thinking I should spend a certain amount on gifts or they might not be seen as desirable or acceptable. Or I get caught in another trap: thinking I need to spend equal amounts on each of our kids as well as matching amounts on each grandchild. Nothing can take the joy and excitement out of gift-giving quicker than materialistic thinking like this. And I'm not alone. Countless other people fall into similar traps during the holiday season.

Maybe we should go back to the simpler days of childhood. Forget about attaching the worth of the gift to its price tag, forget what others think, and give out of spontaneity and love and the pleasure of giving. Go back to offering one another marshmallow Santas and inexpensive figurines. Make our gifts simple, sweet, and satisfying to the soul.

In the same way, whether at Christmas or any time of the year, maybe we should take this simpler approach when considering what we can offer God. After all, most of us probably wonder what, indeed, we have to offer him—the very Creator and King of the universe. But we don't have to worry about it. He's already made it simple.

We don't have to be wealthy or powerful or perfect to give our King the perfect gift. All he wants is us. As a child gives marshmallow Santas to her parents with joy, we can offer our hearts to our heavenly Father with complete confidence. Nothing could make him happier.

So let's reclaim simpler giving today. Let's take back more of the beauty and wonder of the season. Let's relax. Let's give in joy.

That Perfect Christmas Gift

The most wonderful days of the year are here
Joyous days of goodwill and cheer,
The season when love is fondly expressed
And with pure contentment we are blessed.

Our loved ones and friends we have in mind
As we go to any lengths to find
That perfect gift that shows we care,
The depths of our love we long to share.

That gift that's given through sacrifice
The one that shows we paid the price
In time or money or selfless deed
Overwhelms with love, pure love indeed.

It reminds of a love, the purest of all,
That sent a Babe, so tiny, so small,
To be our Savior, to pay the price,
For our sins he became the sacrifice.

That perfect Gift we can never repay
Just believe and accept him, do it today.
Join me in giving him the honor he's due
The perfect gift for him is simply me and you.

"For God so loved the world, that he gave his only begotten Son, that whosoever believeth in him should not perish, but have everlasting life."

John 3:16 KJV

Christmas WISDOM

Take the pressure off and let love, simplicity, and fun guide your Christmas gift-giving.

Christmas PRAYER

Lord, help me more fully give you all my heart and life this Christmas by

Christmas PAST

My earliest memory of trying to give the perfect Christmas gift was when

Christmas PRESENT

Simple, thoughtful gifts that would be especially satisfying to my loved ones this year include

Christmas MERRYMAKING

Hold a Christmas gift-giving brainstorming session with your immediate family. Discuss ways you could make gift-giving more soul-satisfying for your circle of family and friends. Whether simplifying, coming up with a completely different approach, or brainstorming ideas of what might be especially meaningful for each loved one or friend, let love and fun be at the heart of it all. And if it's too late to do something different this year, save your ideas for the future!

8

COME CLOSE TO CHRISTMAS

"O come, let us adore Him, Christ the Lord!"[10]

JOHN FRANCIS WADE

Early in our journey here together, remember reflecting on how, during the Christmas season, most of us feel a deep longing for abiding joy and everlasting light for our souls? And how that longing can only be truly fulfilled by Jesus, by worshiping and adoring our Savior come to us as a newborn Babe? Let's take a closer look at such soul-satisfying worship now.

Yes, we can indeed experience the kind of worship and adoration that will fulfill our deepest Christmas longings. How? We must draw near to our Savior. We must give determined effort and make it our goal to come close to him—to come close to the very core of Christmas.

Over the years as Christmas has approached, I've come close to adore the Savior in a variety of ways. Since I came to know Jesus at an early age, even as a child I felt drawn during December to worship my Savior and King and draw close to the Babe in the manger.

I can still remember traveling home from my grandparents' farms on December Sunday evenings, sitting snug in the warmth of the car as frosty night air covered the countryside. Leaning my head against the back-seat window, I looked up at the stars sparkling like fairy dust against a midnight sky and, with the faith of a child, imagined that holy night in Bethlehem. And as I did, I sang my worship. First one carol and then another, all flowing from a grateful heart—the heart of a child filled with the peace and wonder of the season.

Today I still love to sing my worship. In fact, I carol my way through the Christmas season each year. Actually, I devote time every morning all year long to personal worship. I sing a few praise and worship songs and even some of the old-fashioned hymns I once cut my spiritual teeth on. But during the holiday season? I turn to the traditional Christmas carols for my musical offerings instead.

I start worshiping in song not long after I get up. Singing favorite choruses and carols as I move through my morning routine helps me welcome the Lord into my day and also prepares my heart for a more focused time of worship.

During the holidays my worship time is often spent in front of our Christmas tree. As I soak up its beauty and joy and savor fleeting holy moments that are oh so sweet to the taste, I glance from the tree to our nativity scene to a little lighted church glowing from atop our piano. Oh, what joy these carols and symbols of Christmas celebration inspire in me! What peace descends, like a gentle-falling snow, as I draw near to Jesus. Oh, what wholehearted worship he is due!

I also like to snag opportunities late in the day for a few moments alone to quiet my mind and soul and be refreshed once again by the joy awaiting us in the treasured days approaching Christmas. It's amazing how just a minute or two of gazing at our tree glowing in a darkened room can lower my stress level and soothe my frazzled spirit. I love to look from one favorite ornament to another, especially lingering on the ones that remind me of Christ's birth. As I revel in the glory of that life-changing, miraculous event, my heart swells with thanks and praise. And before I know it, I've come close to Christmas—to Jesus—again.

Drawing near to Jesus during the holidays may look slightly different for you. Some of you may like to meet with him in front of a crackling fire while drinking in the beauty of your Yuletide mantlepiece adorned with family treasures. Candlelight, cinnamon or evergreen aromas, and quiet holiday music may usher others of you into his presence. And some of you may draw closest to Jesus through daily Christmas devotional readings, Advent celebrations, or carrying out family worship traditions.

In whatever ways we reclaim coming close to Christmas—to drawing near to our Savior—he will be thrilled with our efforts and draw near to us as well. That's when we'll find our deep longing for abiding joy fulfilled. Our Savior, who came to us as a little Babe, will fill our hearts with that abiding joy the way nothing and no one else can. And like the Magi, we'll discover that this Babe—King Jesus—is the miracle our hearts truly seek.

Come Close to Christmas

Is the holiday swirling all around you,
Are Christmas plans flooding your mind?
Do you deeply yearn to experience the season,
Its joy and peace to somehow find?

The joy you seek is within your grasp
The peace is not far away,
Stop and take time to approach the manger—
Come close to Christmas this day.

Spend a moment in quiet reflection
Imagine that night once again,
Come close to the manger and adore the Babe
Who holds joy and peace for all men.

Give to him your praise, your cares,
And with your sorrows part,
And if you've not yet given it—
Give to him your heart.

"Come near to God and he will come near to you."

James 4:8 NIV

Christmas **WISDOM**

Make personal Christmas worship a priority and reap the true joy of the season.

Christmas **PRAYER**

Lord, as I come close to the manger and adore you this season, I

Christmas **PAST**

One of my earliest memories of Christmas worship—of me coming close to Christmas—is

Christmas PRESENT

I'd like to deepen my Christmas worship this year by

Christmas MERRYMAKING

Borrow a hymnal from your church and sing (or read) a Christmas carol every day leading up to Christmas. Whether by yourself or with your family, sing all the verses and be blessed by the entire message of the carol. If you're alone, consider the words as if for the very first time and let their message wash over you. If with your family, let each person share the lines of the carol that are the most meaningful to them or a part of it they had never really noticed before.

9

THE CHRISTMAS STAR STILL SHINES

"They looked up and saw a star . . .
And to the earth it gave great light,
And so it continued both day and night."[11]

"THE FIRST NOEL," TRADITIONAL ENGLISH CAROL

IT'S ALL AROUND US. CHRISTMAS. The season of unfettered merriment and joy-filled spirits. It truly is a holly, jolly time of the year—most often. Sometimes, though, life deals us a crushing blow and changes everything. Christmas, as we usually know it and prepare for it, comes to a screeching halt. In mere moments, the holiday season, with all its merry activities and traditions, loses importance to us. No longer is it a priority. Everything has changed.

Unfortunately, sooner or later we'll all undergo times when our Christmas joy gets swallowed up and overtaken by something far more serious than the normal holiday stresses and strains or even the everyday problems of life. Yes, these are life's blows that lay us flat or leave us reeling. Devastating blows. Blows that make a merry Christmas seem impossible.

In 2001, as I wrote the poem included in this chapter, our nation was still grieving the incalculable losses of 9/11. Loss of nearly three thousand precious lives, loss of good health for thousands of others, loss of property and services, loss of jobs, loss of federal funds, as well as our collective loss of feeling safe and secure. Also as Christmas approached that year, a friend from church and her family were living through the horror of losing a young son in an accidental death. For many in our community and in our nation, clouds hung low as joy dimmed to a distant memory that holiday season.

And today? During this Christmas season as I write these words? Longtime friends and neighbors of ours have been thrust into a season of grieving as the wife lost a battle with cancer that took her in only a handful of weeks. For her husband, kids, and grandkids, in the space of a breath, grief fell in its full force. Everything changed. And now, of course, Christmas is different for them this year. Of course, it's outweighed by heartache. I'm grateful Scripture reminds us that "The LORD is near the brokenhearted; he saves those crushed in spirit" (Ps. 34:18). What comfort there is in knowing that when our hearts are breaking, the Lord is near. He will not leave us to suffer alone.

Any number of painful or heartbreaking events can shatter our lives and strip away the joy we normally feel during the Christmas season. As already mentioned, the blow might be the loss of a loved one or come in the form of a national crisis. It may be a divorce or a breakup, a job loss, a frightening diagnosis, the grief of infertility, or possibly a personal failure. Or it could include loss due to a natural disaster, financial ruin, abusive relationships, addictions, or prison time for family members. Finding the merry in a "Merry Christmas" during any of these agonizing situations sounds hopeless, doesn't it?

After all, how does a person go on and live with joy after losing someone they deeply love? Or how does someone recover from the heartrending pain of a broken marriage or other relationship? How do we find hope in the face of an overwhelming diagnosis? How does a couple survive the continual reminders and ongoing pain of infertility? Or how does someone find the courage to break free of an abusive relationship and reclaim their personal worth and hope for the future?

The good news is that comfort, hope, and even the joy of Christmas are not impossible during such dark times. We need only remember that the unparalleled joy of the Christmas story is still true today. We still have a Savior. He still brings light and life to all who believe. We still have hope.

So, my friend, if your heart is broken or bruised, if life has dealt you a blow, look up. The Christmas star still shines. Its hope and comfort never dim. Let the joy Jesus brought on that first Christmas night be your solace and joy today.

The Christmas Star Still Shines

Every Christmas should be celebrated
With carefree abandon and glee,
Every home should shine with joy
As bright as the best Christmas tree.

But maybe this year is different—
Maybe your world's been shaken somehow,
Maybe your joy's not shining as brightly,
Maybe the sun is behind a cloud.

If that's the case in your life today
Why not bow your head in prayer,
Thank God for the things that are constant—
His love, his Word, his care.

He'll brighten the night around you,
Your way will no longer be dim,
For the Christmas star still shines
In the hearts of those who love him.

"And there it was—the star they had seen at its rising. It led them until it came and stopped above the place where the child was. When they saw the star, they were overwhelmed with joy."

Matthew 2:9–10

Christmas WISDOM

When your world is shaken, look for the Christmas star—the light of Jesus. It shines ever for you and me.

Christmas PRAYER

Dear Jesus, will you shine the light of your Christmas star on

Christmas PAST

The Christmas I most needed the comfort, hope, and joy of the Christmas star was

Christmas PRESENT

This year the Christmas star is helping me

Christmas MERRYMAKING

Who do you or your family members know this year who needs a light of comfort and hope for an especially dark time? Brainstorm ways you can gently point them to the Christmas star—to the light of Jesus—and then follow through on one or more of your ideas. Your Christmas joy will be doubled as you bring joy to others.

10

THE CRIES OF CHRISTMAS

"Joy to the world, the Lord is come!
Let earth receive her King."[12]

ISAAC WATTS

In our journey together to reclaim the beauty and wonder of the Christmas season, we've reflected on many of the longings we experience during these magical days. We long for joy, peace, light, and love. We yearn for connection, for merry moments with those we love and moments of wonder over the Babe who changed the world. But Christmas is not only about our longings. God has longings too. And Christmas comes to us, gift-wrapped in those divine yearnings. Some might call them the cries of Christmas.

Yes, like cheerful holiday wrap holding the gift of Christmas itself, the yearnings of God's heart are on display for all to see—or hear—year after year, holiday season after holiday season. Of course, we must slow down long enough to notice them and remember that Christmas at its very heart is the story of Jesus's birth, the story of God's gift of a Savior to a lost and hurting world.

With that in mind, just think of this: God himself had the very first Christmas longings. Before we longed for

Christmas, he created it. Since Adam and Eve's first sin in the garden of Eden, a separation occurred between him—the Holy God—and us—sinful humanity. A payment and forgiveness for our sins were needed to bridge that gulf and restore our relationship.

God longed to remedy the situation. He longed to forgive us. Oh, how his heart ached to give us eternal life with him. We needed a Savior, so God sent Jesus, his only Son, on the most important rescue mission of all time. And when he sent him, he knew that it meant not only his birth as a newborn Babe but his death at the height of his ministry as well.

Jesus would become a sacrificial lamb. Why? God's love and the longing of his heart. These powerful forces compelled him to give such a gift, to make such a sacrifice. "For God so loved the world, that he gave his only begotten Son, that whosoever believeth in him should not perish, but have everlasting life" (John 3:16 KJV). Even before Jesus was born, Zechariah prophesied that salvation would come through the forgiveness of sins because of the tender mercy of God (Luke 1:76–78). And that prophecy came true through Jesus.

What other longings of God might have been at work in his creation of Christmas? He longed not only to forgive us and grant us eternal life, but he longed (and still does!) to be a Father to us and make us his children: "But to all who did receive him, he gave them the right to be children of God, to those who believe in his name" (John 1:12). Why this great privilege? Once again, because of love: "See what great love the Father has given us that we should be called God's children—and we are!" (1 John 3:1).

God also longs for each of us everywhere to hear his cries and respond, for all to believe and receive his gift of salvation. And with Jesus's birth, this good news was indeed announced for all to hear: "But the angel said to them, 'Don't be afraid, for look, I proclaim to you good news of great joy that will be for all the people: Today in the city of David a Savior was born for you, who is the Messiah, the Lord'" (Luke 2:10–11). No news could be better—then or now. Nothing compares.

So how can we fill the longings of God's heart? If we've already believed and become his children, we can renew the giving of our hearts to him by giving every part to him. We can spend time with him in his Word and worship and praise and thank him daily. We can also share the good news with others who still need to hear of the Savior. And if we have not yet answered his cry to believe in him, let this be the Christmas our hearts say *yes*.

Even now, do you hear God's cries? Christmas is calling us. God is pleading with us. What will our answer be?

The Cries of Christmas

Something in us yearns for Christmas,
For contentment, joy, and goodwill,
And so we try to make it happen
Our hearts we hope to fill.

December finds us dashing round
Trying to do the expected things,
But Christmas cries, "There's something more—
Something the Christ Child brings."

Yes, think back to Bethlehem
Recall that night of all nights,
When life was forever changed by his birth
When God's love soared to new heights.

The Son of God—why did he come,
Why leave heaven's glory behind?
He came for you, he came for me,
No greater love we'll ever find.

The Bible teaches we all have sinned
The Savior each of us needs,
So Christmas cries, "Call out to him,
Receive forgiveness—be free!"

*"Believe in the Lord Jesus,
and you will be saved."*

Acts 16:31

Christmas WISDOM

Take time to listen for what God is calling you to do this Christmas—and then say yes.

Christmas PRAYER

Lord, as I listen for your voice this holiday season, please

Christmas PAST

One of my earliest memories of experiencing the wonder of the true meaning of Christmas was

Christmas PRESENT

I will answer God's longing to fellowship with me this Christmas by

Christmas MERRYMAKING

Shop for (or make) a Christmas ornament that will remind you each year of God sending us a Savior so long ago. Consider buying or making extras to share with others, especially with those in your sphere of influence who don't know Jesus as Savior.

11

GIVE THEM THE CHRISTMAS THEY NEED

"Go tell it on the mountain, Over the hills and ev'rywhere;
Go tell it on the mountain That Jesus Christ is born."[13]

"GO, TELL IT ON THE MOUNTAIN,"
TRADITIONAL AFRICAN AMERICAN SPIRITUAL

IT'S NO WONDER CHRISTMAS IS such a beloved holiday season, especially among followers of Christ. Every year for weeks leading up to Christmas Day, we get to celebrate anew the best news ever proclaimed to the world: "Today in the city of David a Savior was born for you, who is the Messiah, the Lord" (Luke 2:11). No wonder the angels cried *glory*. No wonder the shepherds hurried to find the Babe. No wonder they spread the word.

With news like this, it's no wonder *we* still rejoice today, no wonder *we* greet each other with a jolly "Merry Christmas!" With joyful hearts and voices we sing, "Joy to the world, the Lord is come! Let earth receive her King"[14] and "Good Christian men, rejoice with heart, and soul, and voice; Give ye heed to what we say: News! News! Jesus Christ is born today!"[15] And what a privilege to carol, "O tidings of comfort and joy."[16]

Yes, such news, such joy, begs to be shared, to be spread far and wide. This—this is the news people need. And as believers, we have the incredible pleasure and awesome responsibility of continuing to carry that news to others.

Since the day Jesus was born—no, even before—God's chosen messengers have proclaimed this good news. Isaiah the prophet foretold it hundreds of years before God sent our divine Savior. He declared: "The people walking in darkness have seen a great light . . . For a child will be born for us, a son will be given to us . . ." (Isa. 9:2, 6). What an amazing promise he shared! Generations to come clung to these hope-filled words.

Right before the birth of Jesus, God sent angelic messengers to the earthly parents he chose for his beloved Son, the promised Messiah. Scripture tells us the angel Gabriel appeared to Mary and brought her news of the unparalleled privilege God was bestowing upon her: ". . . You will conceive and give birth to a son, and you will name him Jesus. He will be great and will be called the Son of the Most High, and . . . He will reign over the house of Jacob forever, and his kingdom will have no end" (Luke 1:31–33).

An angelic visitor also appeared to Mary's fiancé, Joseph, before Jesus's birth. Since in that time and culture Joseph was already considered her husband, he decided to divorce Mary quietly after he heard news of her pregnancy. He needed a divine directive so he would fulfill his God-ordained role as the earthly father of God's only Son. The angel who delivered the message came to him in a dream and said, "Joseph, son of David, don't be afraid to take Mary as your wife, because what has been conceived in her is from the Holy Spirit. She will give birth to a son, and you are to name him Jesus, because he will save his people from their sins" (Matt. 1:20–21).

Not only angels, but the Holy Spirit himself acted as messenger to John, the preborn forerunner of the Messiah, and to John's mother, Elizabeth, as well. When Mary received her life-changing news, the angel Gabriel also informed her of Elizabeth's miraculous pregnancy. Naturally, Mary rushed to visit her. When she arrived and greeted Elizabeth, Scripture tells us that the baby leaped in Elizabeth's womb when he heard Mary's voice, and that Elizabeth was filled with the Holy Spirit. Immediately, the Holy Spirit revealed Mary's news to her and she exclaimed: "Blessed are you among women, and blessed is the child you will bear! But why am I so favored, that the mother of my Lord should come to me?" (Luke 1:42–43 NIV). Yes, the Holy Spirit spread the news too!

Then on the night of Jesus's birth, God used angels again, but this time with an actual birth announcement. The day that split time, history, and our calendar had arrived. The Savior was born! The most life-changing and glorious news ever proclaimed—the news needed most desperately—rang out from heaven itself through a company of angels to a group of lowly shepherds: "For unto you is born this day in the city of David a Saviour, which is Christ the Lord. . . . Glory to God in the highest, and on earth peace, good will toward men" (Luke 2:11, 14 KJV). "O Holy Night,"[17] indeed!

The shepherds, after running to see the baby for themselves, wasted no time in becoming the next messengers. Undoubtedly, they made sure to tell everyone they saw the most exciting news ever shared. What joy and privilege they must have felt at being eyewitnesses and then heralds of the amazing events.

This great good news all people need has since been proclaimed throughout the ages, from generation to generation. Missionaries, pastors, teachers, family, and friends have faithfully shared the angel's message with those walking in darkness, helping them to see and embrace the Light of the World for themselves.

And now we can reclaim this aspect of the beauty and wonder of Christmas as we fulfill and enjoy the same privilege all the messengers before us experienced. Might God be calling us to share the good news with people in need of the Savior this Christmas? Let's answer his call. Let's be heralds of the best news to ever fall on human ears. Let's give people the Christmas they need.

The Christmas They Need

The holidays are here and people are out
Running their errands and scurrying about,
I notice before long that some are in need
Of a little Christmas spirit, some spirit indeed.

The man who honked rudely and the clerk with a frown
Probably need a little Christmas to turn things around.
As that simple truth takes root in my mind
I realize the Christmas they need is a different kind.

People need more than a magical season
To give their lives meaning, to give their lives reason.
The Christmas they need is the good news of old—
Good news of great joy by an angel first told.

There is a Savior, a Savior for all,
For any who turn to him, for any who call.
His love is for people, all people worldwide,
We are the ones for whom he died.

For those who've not heard of our God of love
His glory is proclaimed by the heavens above,
And he sends his people, the good news they bring
Of the Christmas we need—a Savior, a King!

"As it is written: How beautiful are the feet of those who bring good news."

Romans 10:15

Christmas **WISDOM**

Our words can make an eternal difference in someone's life with each new Christmas season.

Christmas **PRAYER**

My Savior and King, would you please show me how to share the good news with

Christmas **PAST**

During past Christmas seasons, I've shared the good news of a Savior by

Christmas PRESENT

This year I will share in the joy of being a messenger and herald of the Savior by

Christmas MERRYMAKING

Make a list of outreach ministries or projects that share the good news of a Savior with people who are not yet believers. Think of ways you might physically, financially, or prayerfully help join in the outreach and follow through on the ones God nudges you toward.

12

REMEMBERING CHRISTMAS PAST

"When we recall Christmas past, we usually find that the simplest things—not the great occasions—give off the greatest glow of happiness."[18]

BOB HOPE

Back in 1963, Andy Williams declared—with his signature crooner's voice—that Christmas was "the most wonderful time of the year."[19] That sentiment so resonated with people over the years, Americans made the song a Christmas standard. I'm guessing a big part of that sentiment that so captured our hearts is rooted in our memories of Christmas past. Yes, in good old-fashioned nostalgia.

We all have certain holiday activities or traditions that plunge us deep into Christmas memories faster than Santa can slide down the chimney. Making—or eating—fudge is one thing that does it for me. That sweet, chocolatey treat transports me back to childhood days. Back to my earliest memories of extended family gatherings early in the season where I almost always got my first taste of Christmas fudge. It also stirs longings for my mom and memories of how she made fudge each year, creating a family holiday tradition that I've continued and now passed down to my daughters. So, for me, fudge is so much more than a yummy holiday treat. It's about family. Family tradition. Family memories. Family love.

Decorating the tree also brings up cherished memories and nostalgic longings. Playing in the background, favorites like "I'll Be Home for Christmas" and "Let It Snow" help set the stage for memories to spring to life, either of trimming the tree as a kid or of our own girls and their excitement over those magical moments. Add to that the ornaments I treasure, and it's next to impossible *not* to get lost in a sea of nostalgia. Whether heirloom ornaments, gifts from loved ones, vacation mementos, handmade treasures from childhood days, collectibles—and the stories that go with them—or those important firsts and lasts, they all warm my heart. Oh, how I love basking in the beauty and memories of our Christmas tree.

The sights, sounds, smells, and traditions that send nostalgia sweeping through our hearts and minds will be different for each of us. For some it may be lighting Advent candles, inhaling the aroma of freshly baked Christmas cookies, or snow crunching underfoot as their family searches for the perfect Christmas tree at the local tree farm. Others may feel the bloom of nostalgia as they deliver Christmas goodies to neighbors or gather around the piano and sing Christmas carols. Whatever form your visits from Christmas past take, they will leave you with the gift of gratitude for your loved ones and the memories that are yours forever.

And if you're like me, you may even find yourself nostalgic for that very first Christmas in Bethlehem. No, we weren't there when Jesus made his humble entrance into our world or when the host of angels filled the night sky, praising God and proclaiming peace for those on earth. But we know the story well. From generation to generation, it lives on in our hearts as we celebrate the birth of our Savior.

Even now we can reclaim the beauty and wonder of the night that changed the world, of the Savior who's changed our lives. This is the Christmas past that fills our hearts with the longing only he can fill. And this, friends, is the very best kind of Christmas nostalgia.

Christmas Past

Christmas past is ever intertwined
With each new Christmas in my life,
Maybe a sight or simply a sound
Transports me in seconds
Back in time, deep in memory,
To moments cherished and held tightly,
To memories replayed for the joy of it.
The Christmas tree tied to Dad's truck
Freshly cut from a customer's farm,
Our biggest socks for Santa to fill,
Christmas Eve peeks under cover of darkness.
The whole family crammed in the pickup's cab
Traveling through snow and bitter cold
To feast on Grandma's holiday dinner,
To be their family and bring them joy.
This rich store of remembrance never seems to fade
As year after year my mind is flooded
By first one memory that triggers another,
Until my heart is overflowing
With a lifetime of Christmas joy.
My Christmas Past is in fact my Christmas present.

"I remember the days of old;
I meditate on all you have done;
I reflect on the work of your hands."

Psalm 143:5

Christmas WISDOM

Making Christmas memories is well worth the time and investment. They stay with us always.

Christmas PRAYER

Father, as I long to help the very first Christmas live on in my heart and the hearts of my loved ones, help me

Christmas PAST

My earliest Christmas memories are

Christmas PRESENT

As I savor my favorite Christmas memories this year, the list will include

Christmas MERRYMAKING

Set aside an hour or more (as a family or on your own) to look through Christmas photos and videos of past Christmases. Relive the stories surrounding them and enjoy some laughs and tender moments as well.

13

THE SPIRIT OF CHRISTMAS LOVE

"Blessed is the season which engages the whole world in a conspiracy of love!"[20]

HAMILTON WRIGHT MABIE, *MY STUDY FIRE*

If ever there's a time during our calendar year when love and goodwill flow more freely, it's Christmas, isn't it? It's as if someone flips a switch when December dawns and a merry, love-filled current begins surging through the thoroughfares of our hearts and homes, our towns and cities. Christmas is truly the season of miracles, and this kindly "conspiracy of love"—as Hamilton Wright Mabie so aptly dubbed it—shines as one of the best. Indeed, people everywhere give and receive love like they've been loosed from invisible shackles.

Down through the years, people around the world have shared this spirit of Christmas love with others. One dramatic example takes us back to December 1914, during World War I, when the unsanctioned Christmas Truce took place. History tells us that "men from both sides on the Western Front laid down their arms, emerged from their trenches, and shared food, carols, games, and comradeship."[21] If for only a few brief hours, the spirit of love and goodwill that's so prevalent at Christmas rose up and overpowered the very spirit of war. Now that's the spirit of Christmas love.

Many of us remember how Bob Hope, funny man and entertainer extraordinaire, led USO tours abroad during the holiday season just to bring a touch of home to our military personnel stationed overseas. From 1954 through 1990, television viewers across the nation tuned in as Bob and his traveling troupes brought the spirit of Christmas love and joy to American servicemen and women so far from home.[22] Once again, Christmas love found a way.

Of course, certain organizations and programs help us reach out in love beyond our own circles to share the joy of the Christmas season. The Marine Corps' Toys for Tots, Samaritan Purse's Operation Christmas Child, Prison Fellowship's Angel Tree, and The Salvation Army's Red Kettles are just a few of the many outreach efforts that touch the lives of countless families during the days leading up to Christmas. Not only does the spirit of Christmas love compel us to give to those in need, but it compels organizations and ministries to facilitate that giving. Both givers and receivers are blessed when love works with others.

But on an even more personal level, many of us have memories of Christmas love touching our lives in very special ways. The first December both of our girls were away from home in college, our older daughter Kristin surprised us two weeks before Christmas with an impromptu weekend visit just to spend some Christmasy time with us. Since our nest was empty that season, her visit delivered such joy to my homesick-for-my-girls heart. And when Kelli arrived home for Christmas, she bounded in the door several hours earlier than planned, taking me by surprise. The spirit of

Christmas love burst through that door with her, and my squeals of delight welcomed them both.

A couple of years later, about a week before Christmas, we shared Christmas love with an international student attending our local community college. Kayoko and I had been developing a friendship for a few months by that time, so we invited her to our home to see it decorated for Christmas before taking her out for pizza and a drive around town to go light looking.

Each of us enjoyed the entire evening, but the spirit of Christmas love grew from flame to cozy fire twice that night. After showing Kayoko our Christmas tree and sharing the history of some of our most precious ornaments, I pulled a little gift for her out from under the tree. Her eyes lit up and a look of awe softened her features. She said, "We don't place gifts under our Christmas trees in Japan. It's always been my dream to have a present under a Christmas tree!" Was I ever glad I had one for her there that night!

The second moment of Christmas love from that evening will remain forever imprinted on my heart. As Kayoko and I said our goodbyes in front of her apartment building and exchanged a warm hug, I told her, "I love you, Sugar." She said, "I love you too!" Then she stayed there on the sidewalk in the frosty December air—without a coat—and waved as we drove away. What a special opportunity God gave us to share Christmas love that year with someone so far from home.

As we seek to reclaim the beauty and wonder of the season during these days before Christmas, let's be sure to freely give and receive Christmas love. God first lavished it on us by sending us his Son, the Savior we needed, on that night of all nights in old Bethlehem town. Let's accept his gift of love and then heap that spirit of Christmas love on others—in our circles and beyond. May we be part of the love-filled holiday current that sweeps through the world each and every year!

Drawn To Christmas Love

As Christmas Day draws closer
The very atmosphere changes somehow,
The Spirit of Christmas gives us permission
To indulge in love, to let our guard down.

We feel free to smile at strangers
"Merry Christmas" is on our lips,
We take time to chat with children
To talk about Santa's Christmas list.

We're inspired to reach out to others
With a visit, a card, or a call,
We give to those who are in need
Hoping wishes will come true for all.

We're daily drawn to sentimental scenes
Wanting to watch or join right in,
We yearn for joy and Christmas love
Looking for them yet again.

But the Christmas love that's best of all
Comes from the Savior from above,
Let yourself be drawn to him—
Be drawn to Christmas love.

"We love because he first loved us."

1 John 4:19

Christmas WISDOM

Accept Christmas love from above and then pass it on to all you meet.

Christmas PRAYER

Father, when I think of Christmas love, I think of

Christmas PAST

The greatest expression of Christmas love given to me happened when

Christmas PRESENT

I will share love this Christmas by

Christmas MERRYMAKING

Surprise someone who is lonely this Christmas with a loving gift. Anyone who is separated from loved ones for whatever reason will appreciate this more than you know and will remember it always.

14

A NIGHT LIKE NO OTHER

"Christmas is the day which holds all time together."[23]

ALEXANDER SMITH

Some great and pivotal things have happened over the years during the nighttime hours, both in history and in my life as well. Whether Washington's crossing of the Delaware, the *Apollo 11* moon landing, or the fall of the Berlin Wall, each of these events could go down as a momentous night in history. In my personal history, the same could be said of the nights when I graduated high school, got married, became a mom for the first time, or found out I was going to be a grandma—to twins! And twins happened not once, but twice—a set of twins for our other daughter too! Great and pivotal events, indeed.

But none of these events, these nights, can compare with the night the Savior of the world was born. Truly that night was a night like no other before or since.

For as wonderful and miraculous as the birth of any baby is, the birth of Jesus outshines all others. He was not just any baby. Scripture teaches he was the promised Messiah—the Savior of the world: "a Savior was born for you, who is the Messiah, the Lord" (Luke 2:11). Just think of it. On that glorious night—with the Babe's first cries—eternal life and hope were born.

With an event that amazing unfolding on earth, God went a step further to make that night even more unforgettable. He sent messengers from heaven itself to announce the good news. In the middle of an ordinary night, in an ordinary field near the little town of Bethlehem, some ordinary shepherds got the surprise of a lifetime. A heavenly visitor arrived out of nowhere: "Then an angel of the Lord stood before them, and the glory of the Lord shone around them . . ." (v. 9).

After the angel announced the news that would forever change the world, the scene exploded with even more magnificence. "Suddenly there was a multitude of the heavenly host with the angel, praising God and saying: Glory to God in the highest heaven, and peace on earth to people he favors!" (vv. 13–14). The shepherds would count this a night like no other.

But there's more. With the birth of Christ, another great and mighty thing happened that night in Bethlehem. God became man. He became one of us and came to live among us: "In the beginning was the Word, and the Word was with God, and the Word was God. . . . The Word became flesh and dwelt among us (John 1:1, 14). Jesus was indeed Immanuel—God with us—as the angel described him to Joseph in those moments months earlier, when Joseph first found out about the holy child in Mary's womb (Matt. 1:23).

Making that awe-inspiring night even more incredible, we discovered that Jesus not only came to live among us, he came to die for us, to give his life for us, to be the sacrifice for our sins: ". . . the Son of Man did not come to be served, but to serve, and to give his life as a ransom for many" (Mark 10:45). In his great love, the very God of the universe sent his Son to be "the atoning sacrifice for our sins" (1 John 4:10). Yes, God allowed his precious Son, his only Son, to pay for our sins. And Jesus willingly took the punishment that was ours. All for love. All to become our Savior.

Because of Jesus's birth—because of the night like no other—*my* life has been changed. In fact, the lives of all people everywhere have the potential to be changed. For we have not been born into a world without hope, a world where we have no choice but to die in our sins and be eternally separated from God. Instead, we have been born into a world that has a Savior. A Savior longing to give us eternal life and hope. We need only to accept his gift. To accept him as our Savior.

So yes, that long-ago night, that holy night, was truly a night like no other. May all people everywhere allow that truth to also change their lives.

A Night Like No Other

Think back with me, if you will,
To a land and a time far away,
To the night our Savior was born,
To the manger where Jesus lay.

Ponder that night we call holy,
Consider that miracle birth,
Take time to realize the wonder
Of God's love, his Gift, our worth.

Never before and never since
Has there been an equal to that night,
When God himself came down to us
Bringing joy, bringing hope, bringing light.

Because of that night like no other
Life will never be the same
For those accepting the Savior,
For those calling on his name!

*"For everyone who calls on the name
of the Lord will be saved."*

Romans 10:13

Christmas WISDOM

Never lose sight of the miracles and magnitude of Jesus's life-changing birth.

Christmas PRAYER

Dear Jesus, thank you for coming to be my Savior and for leading me to knowledge of you by

Christmas PAST

The magnificent wonder of Jesus's birth as Savior fell fresh on me the Christmas that

Christmas PRESENT

Because knowing Jesus as Savior is life-changing, this Christmas I will

Christmas MERRYMAKING

The birth of Jesus was a brand-new event, unequaled on earth. In the spirit of that newness, enjoy a new-to-you Christmas activity this holiday season. Perhaps you can go caroling in your neighborhood or attend a production of The Nutcracker. Or maybe you've never made peanut brittle, Christmas cut-out cookies, or eggnog. Let this be the year you do so. Try something new!

15

THE CAROLS OF CHRISTMAS

"Sound over all waters, reach out from all lands,
The chorus of voices, the clasping of hands;
Sing hymns that were sung by the stars of the morn,
Sing songs of the angels when Jesus was born!"[24]

JOHN GREENLEAF WHITTIER

O Christmas carol, O Christmas carol, how lovely are your lyrics!

Yes, the carols of Christmas are indeed lovely, in message and melody alike. Personally, they rank high among my all-time favorite songs. I'm guessing that's true for countless other people as well. After all, most of us have heard and sung the carols of Christmas since childhood. They naturally generate a host of warm and fuzzy feelings and, most likely, a multitude of memories as well.

The benefits and blessings of these classic carols so precious to us extend well beyond warm feelings and memories, though. Like gift upon gift, the sweet songs of the season surround us with joy and cover us with peace. Like snowflakes slow dancing their way from heaven, they add grace upon grace to our Christmas celebrations.

The greatest blessing of Christmas carols, however, may lie in their ability to not only lead us to worship but to help us voice our worship as well. Singing these beloved songs in my own private worship time during the holidays always helps me draw close to the Lord and gives me fresh joy and peace year after year. I'll forever love caroling my way to Christmas. The carols of Christmas also allow us to raise our voices in corporate worship—whether in a church service, a musical program, or with a group of carolers. Best of all, as joy fills our hearts through worshiping in song, God delights in our worship. In fact, these may be some of the very times God rejoices over us with singing (Zeph. 3:17). What could be more wonderful?

Another great benefit of the carols comes as we relax and slow down long enough to enjoy listening, humming, or singing along to them. The joy, peace, and pure contentment that result from this happy Christmas activity can provide just the stress relief we need during the hustle and bustle of the holidays. Everyone can use more "all is calm, all is bright" moments as we face the myriad of tasks that clamor for our attention during the Christmas season.

Christmas carols also help us bring our thoughts back to the real meaning of Christmas. At a time when it's so easy to find ourselves caught up in the material aspects of the season, singing and listening to the carols can inspire us to refocus on the miracle and wonder of God's love and Christ's birth. Carols can help us keep our thoughts centered on that great gift. And they will remind us to be among the faithful. To be always coming to him, always adoring him.

On a more festive note, playing favorite carols as background music can instantly set a Christmasy mood. Songs like "Joy to the World" and "God Rest Ye Merry, Gentlemen" can magically transform the atmosphere in your home, workplace, or other settings from that of the daily grind to one with an undercurrent of joy. Why not take advantage of this cheery benefit and enjoy it to the fullest?

Christmas carols also provide us a no-pressure, winsome avenue for sharing the good news of the gospel. Whether caroling, singing with a choir, or playing your favorites at a holiday party or in your neighborhood carpool, listeners will hear about the Savior born for all and be led to consider their own response to this life-giving message. Hopefully, they'll wonder if their hearts have prepared him room or if they've ever fallen on their knees before him in worship. What better Christmas gift than the good news of the Savior can we give to those who don't yet know him?

Not only can we bless unbelievers, we can bless all we encounter as we play and sing the carols of Christmas. The carols will lift spirits, stir up precious memories, help redirect thoughts to that holy night of all nights, and also minister peace, hope, and joy to one and all. No matter where we go—even on social media—as we share the music of Christmas, we can spread goodwill toward everyone just like the host of angels did on that first Christmas night. What joy!

The benefits and blessings of the carols don't stop here. I love how they also generate a spirit of unity and camaraderie among any group who sings them. Remember a few chapters earlier when I referred to enemy soldiers in World War I who laid down their weapons on Christmas Day to enjoy food, carols, games, and comradeship together? Although they came from different countries and cultures, their common experience of celebrating Christmas inspired them to set aside a day to celebrate in unity. One way they could do that was by singing the traditional carols so familiar to all. That same common experience still warms our hearts and unites us in sweet Christmas fellowship wherever we are. We may be at home or away, with loved ones, mere acquaintances, or strangers. It doesn't matter. The carols create an instant bond, another merry miracle of the season—the beauty of unity.

As together we enjoy the unity and camaraderie of singing or listening to the carols of Christmas, we also pass down a fond and time-honored tradition to the next generation. What a blessing to leave them something of real worth as we simply participate in the joyful and worshipful practice of lifting our hearts and voices in praise to the King of kings. Whether singing carols with our families around the piano or Christmas tree, teaching them to a children's choir or Sunday school class at church, or singing with the congregation during a candlelight service, we keep the tradition going, the carols alive. After all, the carols of Christmas tie us to generations past and future.

In addition to all of this, Christmas carols promote pure and simple gratitude. Gratitude for the miraculous gift of the Savior. Gratitude for the amazing and unmerited love of God in sending his Son. And even gratitude for the songs themselves. The music thrills and transports us, the lyrics proclaim truth and inspire us to worship. The appreciation I have for the carols only grows with time.

And finally, the carols of Christmas tell one of the greatest stories ever told—the story of Christ's birth—a story forever worthy of every song, every word written or sung about it. The carols remind us anew of the best news the world has ever heard, helping us each year reclaim the beauty and wonder of the season. "Glory to God in the highest" (Luke 2:14), indeed!

The Carols of Christmas

Christmas and singing go hand in hand
The carols of Christmas across the land,
With joy and wonder we seem to long
To fill this holy season with song.

"O Come, O Come, Emmanuel" we cry
Until your "Angels We Have Heard on High,"
Now "Joy to the World" we gratefully sing
As we celebrate "The Birthday of a King."

Long ago and far away, some shepherds heard
"The First Noel,"
One blessed night, "O Holy Night!" as on their
knees they fell.
"O Little Town of Bethlehem," did you see the star?
Did you ask "What Child Is This?" bringing wise
men from afar?

"Away in a Manger" the Savior slept that night,
The "Sweet Little Jesus Boy" turned darkness into
light.
"Good Christian Men, Rejoice" in this wonderful
news,
"Go, Tell it on the Mountain" for there is no time
to lose!

Let's share the peace, the "Silent Night" of soul
that comes from knowing him,
And when "O Come All Ye Faithful" is heard,
many will join in.
This Christmas let's sing one and all, let's sing far
and near,
Let's make people ask "Do You Hear What I Hear?"

"My heart leaps for joy, and with my song I praise him."

Psalm 28:7 NIV

Christmas WISDOM

Embrace the gift of the glorious Christmas carols God has given us down through the years. Let them enrich your celebration of the season while drawing you ever closer to him.

Christmas PRAYER

Dear Lord, thank you for the carols and music of Christmas. Thank you for

Christmas PAST

My favorite memories of singing, playing, or listening to Christmas carols include

Christmas PRESENT

I will glorify God in song this Christmas season by

Christmas MERRYMAKING

Join with others this Christmas season to spread the "carols of Christmas across the land." Sing in your church or community's Christmas musical or cantata or plan a caroling party for family, friends, neighbors, or coworkers. Include others in brainstorming and planning the details and then have a marvelous time sharing the joy of Jesus's birth with others. You will be a merry holiday blessing to many while being blessed yourself in the process.

16

THE CHRISTMAS GIFTS OF GOD

"How silently, how silently
The wondrous gift is giv'n!
So God imparts to human hearts
The blessings of His heav'n."[25]

—PHILLIPS BROOKS

AS WE CELEBRATE THE HOLIDAYS, I can almost hear the contented sighs and joyful laughter of God. For once again he's busy blessing his children with unexpected gifts designed especially for them. Just as we find joy in giving the perfect gift to someone we love, God must surely delight in giving us perfect gifts too—those sweet surprises or special touches from him we'll remember for a lifetime.

God lavished such a gift on our family the year I wrote the poem featured in this chapter.

Our daughter Kristin and her husband, Shawn, had been wanting a baby for a very long time. And we had been hurting with them for years as they struggled first with infertility and then a lengthy waiting game after they decided to pursue adoption. They finally got the call. A birth mom had selected them! But it wasn't for just one baby—it was for twins! When God finally answered our prayers, he did it beyond our wildest expectations. We couldn't share the news with others until the babies' birth in early January, but our little family rejoiced in this miracle the entire Thanksgiving and Christmas season. Perfect inspiration indeed for my poem that year!

Believe it or not, God gave us another miracle Christmas gift the next year. We didn't find out about it, however, until a few days after Christmas. Our younger daughter Kelli and her husband, Jake, had also been dealing with infertility. She finally became pregnant but miscarried almost immediately. Amid crushing disappointment, they decided to take a break from fertility efforts during the November and December holidays. I began pleading, "Lord, please bless them with a Christmas miracle." And unbeknownst to me, their pastor prayed with them as well in early December. Then right before Christmas, Kelli felt different—she felt pregnant! But she didn't breathe a word until after Christmas when her pregnancy test showed positive. God had given them—and us—the Christmas miracle we all longed for!

The miracle didn't stop there, though. By late January, Kelli's sonogram showed the full extent of the miracle. Twins! That's right, another set of twins for our family! Bubbling over with this news of twins again, I told everyone, "God is just plain showing off!" Miracle answers to prayer two years in a row. Double, double Christmas gifts of God!

Not every Christmas gift of God will be as jaw-dropping as twin babies, but that doesn't diminish their impact or our gratitude. Gifts designed by God especially for us always carry an air of the miraculous. The Christmas following my mom's unexpected death, my sister Carolyn had already drawn Mom's name for the gift exchange. On

Christmas day, Dad opened the gift—a Christopher Radko ornament given in Mom's honor to add to her collection. Mom especially enjoyed collecting the churches, and she would have loved the one Carolyn chose for her.

Little did I know, God had one of the very same Radko ornaments waiting for me at a nearby Dillard's. When my sisters and I made our traditional trek to the after-Christmas sale, I spotted it. It was the only one left in the store. Having already started my own collection, I said, "Carolyn, Janice, look! I have to get it!" It would forever remind me of Mom and that first Christmas without her. A precious Christmas gift from God especially for me. I'll treasure it always.

Sometimes a Christmas gift from God will come in the form of a fun surprise. Remember the one I previously mentioned when Kristin was in college and made an impromptu visit home in mid-December? She was yearning for some Christmas togetherness and time at home, and oh, how it hit the spot for me too. It was my first Christmas without either of my girls living at home, and my heart ached with lonesomeness for them. Kristin's visit provided the cure we both needed.

Then right before Christmas that same year, you may remember how I told you that God surprised me again. Hours before Kelli's scheduled arrival home from college, she breezed through the back door with eyes twinkling and a smile as big as a kid's on Christmas morning. "Kelli!" I gasped. "You're home! Early!" I wrapped her in hugs as we laughed and talked faster than Santa's reindeer streaking through the sky. How God must have been chuckling as he watched us. He knew how much this momma's heart needed surprises like these that year. In other words, Christmas gifts straight from God.

Other times, God's Christmas gifts to us come about as we try to be a Christmas blessing to someone else. One Christmas Eve when our girls were home from college, we went to visit my husband's mother at the assisted living complex where she lived. Before we left, we went to the commons area and Kristin, our piano major, sat down at their piano and treated her grandma and another lady sitting there to a mix of holiday tunes and Christmas carols. Smiling, the woman said, "I've been hoping all day that someone would come and play Christmas music. Young lady, you absolutely made my Christmas Eve." What a gift to all of us to be a blessing to someone we didn't even know. I'm also reminded of that time when I had a present under our tree for our international student, Kayoko, and how it had always been a dream of hers to have a gift under a Christmas tree. To provide that kind of dream-come-true for her blessed me beyond words. Another Christmas gift from God, for sure!

God has also given me some priceless Christmas gifts through moments of sweet fellowship with family and friends. One Christmas years ago during one of our family Christmas concerts at Mom and Dad's, we had all gathered near the piano to enjoy our concert time. After Kristin, a college senior at the time, and our young niece Joanna played a few duets, several of us stood around the piano and lifted our voices in a merry sing-along. Joanna and our nephew Cody, both just grade-schoolers at the time, sang out, faces beaming with joy. Our hearts glowed as well, and the family togetherness we experienced topped any gift we might find under the tree.

Singing the carols of Christmas with my writers group at our Christmas parties over the years has brought great joy as well, and the fond fellowship shared among our church family during and following Christmas Eve candlelight services has warmed countless hearts over the years. All of these and other moments of love shine as some of the most cherished gifts from God.

But the best gift, the matchless Christmas gift of God, came to us over two thousand years ago when Jesus arrived as a newborn Babe. God gave him to us, one and all, to save us from our sins if we will but ask him to be our Savior. And this, friends, is a gift we can enjoy for all eternity.

The Christmas Gifts of God

You may not find them under the tree
They may not sparkle with bows,
But the Christmas gifts of God will shine
Much brighter than jewelry or clothes.

For the gifts of God come custom-wrapped
Just for me and you,
Answered prayers, sweet surprises,
And even a miracle or two.

But God gave the greatest gift to us
The night he sent his Son,
A Savior born for one and all
New life, new hope begun.

And now this Christmas season
With God's love so deep and broad,
Let's open our hearts and hands to receive
The Christmas gifts of God.

"Every good and perfect gift is from above."

James 1:17

Christmas WISDOM

Be on the lookout for God's gifts to you this Christmas—the special touches, the answered prayers, and yes, perhaps even a miracle.

Christmas PRAYER

Father, how can I ever thank you for

Christmas PAST

The Christmas gifts God has given me that stand out the most clearly in my memory are

Christmas PRESENT

This year God has

Christmas MERRYMAKING

Start a Christmas Gifts of God journal, either on your own or with your family. Record some of his special gifts from past Christmases or simply start with this year. Add entries to it each year and watch your Christmas joy grow!

17

THE SWEETEST SOUNDS OF CHRISTMAS

"It is Christmas in the heart that puts Christmas in the air."[26]

WILLIAM T. ELLIS

CHRISTMAS IN THE AIR REALLY does spring from Christmas in the heart, doesn't it? Our warm smiles as we wish others "Merry Christmas," the twinkle in our eye as we plan for surprises and try to keep them secret, the kind deeds done in offering help to others. All these gestures of the heart help create that magical Christmas-in-the-air atmosphere we love so much. But the sounds of Christmas themselves play a major role in this festive mood as well. Sounds that not only hold treasured memories from bygone days but also help us live out new memories today. Classic sounds—sweet sounds—of yesterday, today, and always.

Think of some of the most basic sounds that signal Christmas is here. Several will capture our attention even before Thanksgiving has come and gone. Strains of holiday music wafting through the air and the sound of bells ringing top the list. Jingle bells, church bells, Salvation Army Red Kettle bells, and doorbells as packages are delivered. Even store-entry bells tinkling at a quick pace as customers come in to shop. All of these begin early in the season.

Talk of Santa and Christmas lists gets added to the mix soon after, and as Thanksgiving gives way to Black

Friday and the dawn of December, greetings of "Merry Christmas" begin to meet us as we go. The sound of our favorite Christmas movies and classic TV shows playing in our homes offer us the comfort and joy that come with tradition. And as the days get colder, the crunch of snow and crackling fires add a perfect touch to the holiday atmosphere. All these sounds are sweet to our ears because they're associated with everything Christmas and a lifetime of holiday memories.

Add the merry sounds of family next and hear the soundtrack of Christmas take on a whole new layer of holiday joy. As the tree gets decorated, laughter and reminiscing abound—along with a few little disagreements over which ornament goes where. All of this, of course, while "Rockin' Around the Christmas Tree" and other holiday favorites play in the background.

Parents and grandparents can also be heard reading Christmas stories to the kids and teaching them the songs youngsters love so much like "Rudolph the Red-Nosed Reindeer" and "Santa Claus Is Coming to Town." Sounds of baking and candy-making drift out of the kitchen while children's excited voices echo throughout the house. The whisper of secrets snags everyone's interest, while the rattle of wrapping paper and bows signals the tree will soon hold secrets of its own.

When it's time for presents, each recipient adds their exclamations of surprise, joy, and thanks to the gift-opening gaiety. And finally, when visitors begin to head home, the shared expressions of "I love you" warm our hearts long after the words ring out. Yes, the sweet sounds of family during Christmas surely rank among the most joyful of all.

The sound of friends also magnifies the merry in the soundtrack of the season. The mixing, mingling, and music at holiday parties thrill our ears and our spirits as well. Wishes of "Merry Christmas" seem especially dear as parties wind down and friends go their separate ways.

And oh, the joy we experience when we share laughter and conversation with our dearest friends as we go on Christmas outings together. Whether shopping, caroling, or meeting somewhere for our favorite holiday drinks or desserts, their precious voices bless us with a gift we can carry always in our memories. Then there are times the sound of surprise visitors brightens our holidays in a special way as neighbors or friends drop by with holiday goodies or other thoughtful gifts.

The Babe of Bethlehem's birth has also given rise to a variety of beloved sounds as we celebrate our Savior each year. Choirs start practicing their Christmas cantatas long before the season officially arrives. As Christmas draws a little closer, play practice for the kids begins in earnest. Moms and dads everywhere can be heard running lines with their kiddos or listening as they rehearse their musical numbers. Seeing and hearing it all come together on performance day brings joy to one and all.

Special church services like the Hanging of the Greens, Advent celebrations, and even our regular December worship services add such joyous sounds to the season. Multiply that with holiday activities like caroling in neighborhoods, hospitals, senior living facilities, and nursing homes. Angel Tree visits and outreach in shelters also add a compassionate and more serious layer to the sounds of the season—though certainly a bittersweet layer. But bringing hope to the hurting is a sweet sound of Christmas as well, isn't it?

Finally, consider the sounds so sweet to the Lord himself during this special time of year. Hearing and watching the kind deeds we do for one another must make him beam with pride and joy, and the prayers we offer for blessings for others must meet his ears like a beautiful melody. And how his heart must delight in our voices raised in corporate worship as we sing the carols of Christmas.

The sounds of our personal Christmas worship must also touch the Lord's heart with a tenderness one only feels for their dearly loved children and grandchildren. And when he hears us sharing the good news of a Savior born for all, his heart surely fills with joy and the anticipation of another who might draw close to him.

But the sweetest sound comes when someone calls on him and offers his heart in believing faith. When someone says, "I need you, Jesus. Please forgive me and be my Savior."

Yes, we can reclaim much of the beauty and wonder of the season as we listen for and rejoice in the sweetest sounds of Christmas. The sounds that stir our hearts. The sounds of yesterday, today, and always.

The Sweetest Sounds of Christmas

Listen this Christmas,
Tune your ear,
And the season's sweet sounds
You soon will hear.

Hear the bells jingling,
Hear the crunch of the snow,
While the fire's cozy crackle
Soothes spirits in its glow.

Christmas music all around
Fills hearts with peace and joy,
Whether songs of snow, songs of home,
Or songs of a Baby Boy.

Wishes of "Merry Christmas"
Greet us throughout the day,
Friends, neighbors, loved ones,
Even strangers along the way.

Children's excited voices
The sound of secrets being told
Are joined by hearty welcomes
Inviting all in from the cold.

Hear the priceless laughter
As family traditions are carried out,
Timed photos and Christmas movies
Will be included without a doubt.

The sounds of giving and receiving
Make us smile, they warm the heart,
Sweet "Thank yous" echo in our ears,
That's the very best part.

Voices of friends and family
All together for Christmas this year,
Silenced only by the Christmas story
So full of wonder, so dear.

As the story unfolds we can almost hear
The newborn Babe's first cry,
And then the angels' songs of glory
Filling that Holy Night sky.

Our praise today must thrill Christ so,
Must fill his heart to the brim,
But the sweetest sound is someone saying,
"I'll give my heart to him."

"Praise our God, all peoples, let the sound of his praise be heard."

Psalm 66:8 NIV

Christmas **WISDOM**

Take time to tune your ears for the sounds of Christmas surrounding you this season.

Christmas **PRAYER**

Lord, help me add to the sweet sounds of Christmas this year by

Christmas **PAST**

The sounds of Christmas I remember the best from my childhood were

Christmas PRESENT

My favorite sounds of Christmas so far this year have been

Christmas MERRYMAKING

Join with friends or family to deliver the merry sounds of jingle bells—along with a surprise gift—to others this Christmas season. Get those bells jingling as you approach the front doors of their homes. When they open the door, watch the joy and surprise on their faces as you call out, "Merry Christmas," and hand them an unexpected gift. Possibilities might include a beautiful poinsettia, a plate of Christmas goodies, a loaf of your favorite holiday bread, a tin of popcorn, or even a gift basket of groceries if you know someone in need. What other ideas would you add? Have fun playing Santa!

18

TOUCHING BABY JESUS IS STILL POSSIBLE TODAY

"What religion ever had a god that wanted such intimacy with us . . . What God ever came so tender we could touch Him?"[27]

ANN VOSKAMP

I LOVE HOW GOD SENT our Savior to us as a tiny baby, born to young newlyweds of humble means. He didn't send him as a mighty king in all his glory or even as a newborn prince to a royal couple. Either would have seemed out of reach to most people. No, God sent us a Savior we could all approach, one we could all be easily drawn to. A precious, winsome baby we'd long to get a glimpse of. After all, we naturally want to gather around a newborn. To gaze with wonder and joy at the new life before us, to reach out and get even the tiniest touch of this little miracle. God certainly knew what he was doing when he sent Jesus to the world like this, didn't he?

Today Jesus is no longer a baby, but we don't have to feel left out of approaching the manger to adore him there. We can still reach out and touch him. Still express our wonder and joy. Still show him our love.

We can come close to Jesus today through our worship. Even now, in our hearts and minds we can draw near the

Babe. And oh, how we will touch his heart when we do. We can imagine him cradled in the manger before us, with his adoring parents, the awestruck shepherds, and devoted angels looking on from the heavenly realm. Yes, friends, we can worship and adore him.

We can touch Jesus's heart in another way as well this Christmas season. In the days leading up to his crucifixion, Jesus spent time in Jerusalem with his disciples and taught them many things. At one point he said, "Truly I tell you, whatever you did for one of the least of these brothers and sisters of mine, you did for me" (Matt. 25:40). What does this mean for us today?

What if it means that during this special time of celebrating his birth—and all throughout the year—we can touch the heart of Jesus by reaching out in love? By touching those in need or those seen as less-than in the world's eyes. Isn't it wonderful to know we can do this? What a gift others give us when they allow us to show them love and care. And what a gift we give others when we receive their loving gesture.

I've been on the receiving end myself when others have touched Jesus's heart and served him by helping me or my loved ones during the holiday season. One Christmas when Kristin was just eight years old, both she and my husband Don came down with a stomach bug early Christmas morning. Our hearts sank as we realized we'd miss the long-anticipated family celebration at Mom and Dad's that day. The whole family couldn't be at our Christmas gathering the year before, but this year the entire gang was coming. We would be stuck seventy-five miles away from everyone. Our Christmas reunion would be ruined.

Suddenly I remembered all the dinner items and special treats I had ready to take with us. "Oh, no!" I said. "I've got all that food Mom is counting on for today." Not only would we be absent, but a good portion of Christmas dinner would be missing as well, not to mention the holiday goodies for the following days. After bemoaning our situation together and wondering what we should do, Don said, "Cheryl, you and Kelli should go on and take the food. Kristin and I will surely be better by tomorrow and can drive over then." After several protests, I agreed to this unhappy but sensible solution. My heart broke, though, leaving half my family at home and sick on Christmas Day.

When we arrived at Mom and Dad's, questions started flying. I relayed our pathetic tale to cries of "Oh, no!" nearly uttered in unison. The glorious Christmas reunion we'd all planned didn't feel so glorious anymore. We went on with Christmas dinner, but Don and Kristin's absence left our usual festive spirits subdued—until midway through the meal when talk of a rescue mission arose. "Keith, I think after dinner we should drive over to Coffeyville and pick up Don and Kristin," Dad announced.

"Sounds like a good idea to me," my brother-in-law Keith answered nonchalantly, trying not to smile. Merry energy zipped through our group over this Christmas rescue plan. As soon as we finished dinner, Dad called Don to make sure he and Kristin were on the upswing before putting the plan into motion. When he got off the phone, all eyes turned to him. With a big smile he said, "Let's go, Keith!" Everyone cheered.

The heroes arrived back with their charges by 5:00 p.m. and our real Christmas reunion commenced. Kristin still looked a little pale but happy. She will never forget the Christmas her grandpa and Uncle Keith came to get her and the love that sent them on their rescue mission. Not unlike another Hero who came for us more than two thousand years ago. Love sent Jesus on his rescue mission too. He reached out to us so we can now reach back to him. We can touch his heart with our worship. Touch his heart by reaching out to "the least of these." And sometimes "the least of these" is family.

Not only have I been on the receiving end as someone's love touched Jesus's heart during the holidays, but by his grace, I've been on the giving end as well. As a child, I remember our family driving through snow and bitter cold on Christmas Day to reach my grandparents, alone on their farm and waiting for the joy we would bring them. As an adult with children of my own, I hustled our little gang out the door a day early one year—after a few hours of frantic packing—to strike off cross-country and outrace an ice storm. Once again, to bring Christmas joy to some who were alone. When we arrived, my sister Debbie's family appeared in their doorway, beaming as we piled out of our car. Both big adventures done in love required effort and discomfort at times, but what joy we all reaped.

I've shared previously about the wonderful Christmas memories created while reaching out several years ago to our international student, Kayoko. Touches of love given through time, friendship, gifts, and ultimately sharing the good news of our Savior not only moved her but must have touched Jesus's heart too. I also showed love to precious one- and two-year-olds as a Sunday school teacher, sharing the story of Jesus's birth each December for over thirty years. Might the Lord see little children as some of "the least of these" (Matt. 25:40)? I imagine so.

So how might we touch the heart of Jesus this Christmas? We can do it daily through our personal worship, enjoying these special days with our Lord as we focus on him, the Babe in the manger. And we can do it as we reach out in love “to the least of these”—and also let others love us as God leads them.

Personal, custom-fit opportunities will present themselves to you just as they have to me over the years, but many opportunities common to all will be available to us as well. We might go caroling at a retirement village or visit someone who is homebound or alone. We may even know a couple or a family who can’t be with any of their other family members over the holidays, or perhaps we know someone whose season is anything but joyous this year and desperately needs a loving touch.

Some will find an opportunity to serve at a homeless shelter or soup kitchen. Others will prepare gift boxes for *Operation Christmas Child*, buy or deliver gifts for Angel Tree children, or donate food for Christmas baskets given to those in need. Many of us can drop a few dollars in the Salvation Army Red Kettles and give charitable donations to ministries and organizations who serve the poor or those in prison. There are so many avenues available! We’ll certainly find a few that move us to give.

May we not neglect this aspect of reclaiming the beauty and wonder of the Christmas season. Let’s touch Jesus’s heart with our adoring worship. Let’s touch his heart by touching others with our love—with his love. Oh, how he will be blessed. How he will cherish our tender touch.

Touching Baby Jesus

Close your eyes and journey back
To history's most holy night,
Imagine the Babe that changed the world
Imagine those drawn to his light.

His parents the first to look on his face
The first to touch the divine,
The first to kiss his tiny cheek
To see his glory shine.

The animals sharing the stable that night
Must have watched the miracle birth,
They must have drawn near to nuzzle the Babe
To touch heaven come to earth.

The shepherds, the first to hear the news,
Arrived breathless in wonder and joy,
With tender touch they must have reached out
To this Savior, this baby boy.

Now it's your turn to approach the manger
Jesus is calling, "Will you draw close?"
How will you answer, what will you do?
Reach out and touch—he'll be reaching to you.

"Let us then approach God's throne of grace with confidence."

Hebrews 4:16 NIV

Christmas WISDOM

Let's not neglect the opportunity to touch the heart of Jesus and serve him this Christmas season.

Christmas PRAYER

Jesus, my heart yearns to

Christmas PAST

I've touched the heart of Jesus during past Christmas seasons when

Christmas PRESENT

This Christmas I will reach out and touch Jesus's heart by

Christmas MERRYMAKING

On your own or with loved ones, think of one of "the least of these" (Matt. 25:40) known to you. Plan a time you could see that person to reach out to him or her with a loving touch—a handshake, a hug, or a pat on the shoulder, along with the gift of time, concern, or a need met and joy delivered. Maybe you're thinking of a single mom in your neighborhood or workplace who is struggling to make ends meet. Maybe someone you see regularly at the homeless shelter where you volunteer or perhaps a little child at your church who seems in need of some loving attention. Reach out in love to whomever the Lord brings to mind or places in your path.

19

A REFUGE FOR CHRISTMAS

"God rest ye merry, gentlemen;
Let nothing you dismay.
Remember Christ our Saviour
Was born on Christmas Day . . .
O tidings of comfort and joy,
Comfort and joy."[28]

"GOD REST YE MERRY, GENTLEMEN,"
TRADITIONAL ENGLISH CAROL

Some years when the Christmas season dawns, all we want is a refuge from the storms of life. We can't muster the desire to trim a tree or decorate our homes in picture-perfect holiday style, much less rack our brains for the perfect gifts for everyone on our Christmas lists. All we want is a haven of rest and peace from the stress or heartache that's engulfing us. We long for a place of comfort, a safe harbor.

In 2020, the year I wrote the poem included in this chapter, the worldwide COVID pandemic had upended everyone's lives and worn us out in every way. We couldn't even celebrate Christmas as we normally would. In our nation alone that year, COVID had not only sickened more than twenty million people and claimed the lives of more than

350,000,[29] but hospitals and medical personnel faced crises like never before. The economy staggered as businesses took heavy blows, while employees were laid off, losing income.

Debate and division on how to best deal with the pandemic marked our nation from the White House and halls of Congress all the way down to local officials. Even to our own families and friends, mine included. Such had been our lot—our lives—for nearly the entire year. By December, hearts everywhere cried out for refuge. For the pandemic to be over. For peace and rest, for love and comfort and joy. Thank God our family had not lost a loved one, but the pain of social distancing and separations cut deep. Ah, for the refuge of life back to normal.

A pandemic doesn't have to strike, though, for us to yearn for a refuge at Christmastime. Less than ten years into our married life, heavy burdens on both sides of our family during one holiday season weighed us down and robbed us of our usual joy. Serious illness for one family member and an especially troubling period for another hovered like dark storm clouds. If only the burdens could magically disappear.

Fast-forward to December 2001, to a heartrending period I mentioned in an earlier chapter. A time when our nation still reeled from the 9/11 terrorist attacks. We didn't personally know anyone killed that day or any who lost loved ones during those horrendous hours, but our sense of safety had been stripped away. Also, my heart ached for the thousands grieving for loved ones whose places were empty that Christmas season. Add to that the tragic and accidental death of a young son to a family we knew, and the reality of unbearable grief hit even closer to home. So many people needed a refuge from the pain of a broken heart that year.

Twelve years later the holiday season found me with a broken heart of my own. We had lost my mom unexpectedly several weeks earlier due to injuries sustained in a car accident. As I decorated our home and tree that year, strains of "Silver Bells," "Silent Night," and other Christmas favorites left my heart aching with memories and longing for Mom. I grieved her loss with each ornament I hung that reminded me of her. However, a lifetime of happy Christmas memories she helped create for me balanced that ache with gratitude. It was a bittersweet time to be sure. How I thanked God for my precious mom—and for strengthening me for each new day without her. However, moments of deep grief and even anger at how a person can just disappear from this world still crept in that holiday season and left me needing the solace of a refuge. But my faithful heavenly Father comforted me again and again during those days and through the weeks and months that followed.

The next year during the Christmas season, an unexpected new challenge and a very different reason for craving a refuge turned our lives upside down. In mid-November my husband fell roof-high from a ladder, fracturing his spine in several places and also breaking a rib. His injury impacted every part of our lives for weeks on end.

As Don dealt daily with serious pain and the discomfort of wearing a back brace 24/7, I endured the most stressful Christmas season of my life up until that point. Caring for Don and doing everything that needed to be done for life in general, plus preparing for Christmas, demanded all I had and more. Yes, I needed a refuge.

A few times refuge came in the form of much-needed help from our daughters when they could be with us. Other times it came by different means—errands of mercy by friends, thoughtful gifts from near and far, medical advice from nurses we knew, or visitors dropping by for a few minutes. And undergirding it all, stood a multitude of people praying faithfully for us.

The examples from my life form only the tip of an iceberg of serious problems borne by countless people each holiday season. Right when everyone should be savoring the most wonderful time of the year, many instead struggle with overwhelming situations that are anything but wonderful: national crises, losses of all kinds, serious illness and pain, caregiving demands, or perhaps infertility, divorce, abuse, prodigal children, poverty, or homelessness. Thousands of people yearn simply for a refuge for Christmas. A place of peace. A shelter from life's storms.

Are you in need of a refuge this Christmas? Look to the manger. Look to Christ. Unmatched rest, refreshment, and hope await us in him. Join me, won't you? Let's reclaim this priceless part of the beauty and wonder of the season.

A Refuge for Christmas

Some seasons of life—some years—
Test us to our limits and beyond,
And a refuge for Christmas is all we want
From the moment December dawns.

No longer drawn to material things
Our hearts now long for rest,
For love and peace, for comfort and joy,
For safety and freedom from all stress.

Oh, in that refuge let us find
Our loved ones gathered near,
Talking, laughing, playing together,
Thanking God for Christmas cheer.

And as we think on Christmas cheer
We see Christ's holy light,
And realize true refuge is found in him
For Christmas and for all of life.

So let's rest in him this Christmas
For he's still the Savior for all,
Giving love, peace, comfort, and joy,
Being our refuge when we call.

"The eternal God is your refuge, and underneath are the everlasting arms."

Deuteronomy 33:27 NIV

Christmas WISDOM

The Lord is our ultimate refuge when we hurt during the holidays—or any day of the year.

Christmas PRAYER

Lord, this year—and each Christmas season—help me remember that

Christmas PAST

I most needed a refuge for Christmas the year that

Christmas PRESENT

This Christmas I need a refuge as I

Christmas MERRYMAKING

Think of a way you might provide a breath of refuge for someone going through a tough time this holiday season. Maybe you can share love, peace, comfort, or joy by inviting them to attend a candlelight service with you or to join your family on Christmas Eve or Christmas Day. Perhaps you could deliver a fragrant wreath, centerpiece, or a favorite scented Christmas candle. Or drop off a home-cooked meal or some of your special Christmas goodies. If it's earlier in the season and you know someone who's simply not up to decorating their tree or home this year, give of your time and do it for them—or with them. Your loving gesture will minister to them for weeks. Whatever your idea, the moments of refuge you provide will mean the world and point them to Jesus, our true refuge.

20

DIVINE DELIVERY

"This is the Lord of the universe come down to be with . . . you."[30]

JONI EARECKSON TADA

THE TIME-SPLITTING, WORLD-CHANGING, LIFE-ALTERING EVENT that became known as Christmas was the miracle all humankind needed. A sinful people separated from a holy God needed a Savior, needed a miracle. So the Lord of the universe—Jesus, Immanuel, God with us—came to live among us, to die for us, to pay for our sins and be our Savior.

Yes, God's provision of a Savior came in the person of his son Jesus, the Messiah, sent to us as a baby. Birthed from a divine conception. Heralded by angels. Welcomed and worshiped by low and high alike. He was Christ the Lord. The miracle—the divine delivery we needed. As Joni Eareckson Tada said, the baby Jesus was the God of the universe come down to be with . . . us.

Just think of other miracles that have happened down through the ages. They've brought God's power to bear on our lives and situations. They've brought his life-giving, life-altering changes. They, too, have brought divine delivery.

Consider the scriptural accounts of miracles Jesus did during his brief years of ministry on earth. You will find them in the Gospels of Matthew, Mark, Luke, and John.

Jesus performed miracles of provision like changing the water into wine at a wedding banquet. Or feeding thousands of people from five small loaves and two small fish. Or blessing the disciples with nets bulging with fish after hours and hours of no luck.

Jesus displayed his power over nature as well when he calmed a storm, when he walked on water, and when he made a fig tree wither. He also showed his power over the spirit world, casting demons out of those they possessed.

And of course, Jesus also performed numerous healing miracles. Everything from healing the blind, the deaf, the mute, and the crippled to those suffering from leprosy, fever, dropsy, bleeding, or deformity. He even gave life back to the dead when he raised Jairus's daughter, the widow's son at Nain, and his good friend Lazarus.

Through the Scriptures we see time and again the miracles Jesus bestowed while he walked the earth. Divine deliveries imparted during times of need, danger and fear, illness and affliction, and hopeless situations. In fact, after his crucifixion, Jesus himself rose from the dead, providing the ultimate victory over death and Satan—the divine delivery we needed from sin, the divine delivery from the eternal punishment that would be ours if not for our Savior. We need only believe and accept his gift.

The final miracle witnessed from Jesus's days on earth happened as he ascended to heaven while blessing the disciples. Isn't it fitting that the Son of God came to earth through a divine delivery and then left it through another one? His story—his entire life—how utterly amazing!

God's divine deliveries didn't stop when Jesus went back to heaven, though. God continued to grant miracles through the apostles during those early days of the church. The book of Acts contains one supernatural act after another. Everything from the day of Pentecost when the disciples spoke in various languages unknown to them, to healings, to casting out demons, to signs and wonders. Paul—by God's power—even raised a young man from the dead.

God also provided divine deliveries during that period through events like Peter's miraculous escape from prison. Another time, an earthquake opened prison doors and loosed the chains of Paul and Silas, allowing them to witness to the jailer. God also spared Paul's and his shipmates' lives during a disastrous shipwreck. And then shortly afterward, a poisonous snake bit Paul but no harm came to him. All miracles. All more divine deliveries for people, from God.

Miracles didn't stop with the early church and the apostles either. God is still blessing with divine deliveries. Every generation of people across every continent could recount examples of God's miraculous intervention in their lives. We've all seen or heard of healing miracles, either instantaneously or through medical treatment. Many have witnessed miracles of deliverance from drugs, smoking, pornography, or other addictions. And we must not forget the miracles of forgiveness, restored relationships, and God's peace, comfort, and hope in times of turmoil and grief.

God has indeed come down to be with us and bring his power to bear on our lives through such miracles. What's more, every person who has ever come to Christ for forgiveness and cleansing from sin is a miracle. Each of us has experienced God's divine delivery.

Are you in need of a miracle this Christmas? Ask the Lord of the universe to touch your life with his power. Or perhaps you need to ask on behalf of a family member or friend. Ask and then trust him for the divine delivery he knows is best. And most of all, remember: God has already given us the miracle we truly need. He's given us a Savior. He's given us himself.

Divine Delivery

This time of year I hear echoes
Of angels on parade,
When God sent his Son as a newborn Babe
When a divine delivery was made.

No gift before or since
Can match our Savior's birth,
Except the divine delivery from sin
His blood shed for all on this earth.

But as we make our way through life
God's miracles we still need,
His hand, his help through our heartaches,
Precious divine deliveries indeed.

So if any among you are hurting today
And need to know hope lives,
Just lift your eyes and hearts to God,
For divine deliveries he still gives.

"He performs wonders that cannot be fathomed, miracles that cannot be counted."

Job 9:10 NIV

Christmas **WISDOM**

God is still the God of miracles.

Christmas **PRAYER**

Lord, as I think about divine deliveries needed today, please hear my prayers for

Christmas **PAST**

The divine delivery—or deliveries—I will never forget happened when

Christmas PRESENT

A divine delivery I've already seen, experienced, or heard about this Christmas season is when

Christmas MERRYMAKING

Could you and your loved ones be part of a divine delivery by giving anonymously to someone you know who's in great need this Christmas season? If it's a financial need, perhaps your gift—whether monetary or in goods—could be delivered by your pastor, a mutual friend, or an acquaintance sworn to secrecy. If the longed-for miracle is a desperate need to be with a certain loved one, maybe you could work behind the scenes logistically and financially to make that divine delivery happen. If the need is for something you can't provide, think of a creative way to show your support. The emotional lift you give could be the divine delivery of love this person or family needs to see them through this Christmas season.

21

BOUNDLESS CHRISTMAS PRAISE

"Then let us all, with one accord,
Sing praises to our heav'nly Lord . . .
Noel, Noel, Noel, Noel;
Born is the King of Israel."[31]

"THE FIRST NOEL,"
TRADITIONAL ENGLISH CAROL

DO YOU FEEL IT? THE charge in the air? The rush of excitement that tells us Christmas is almost here?

The final days are upon us. The countdown days leading up to the glorious celebration of the day the world forever changed. Many families have begun to gather as love fuels them on their way to one another. We're all giving last-minute finishing touches to our homes, our Christmas trees, our pantries while our Christmas joy and praise begin a mighty crescendo now. A continual praise springs from our hearts as we meditate on the magnitude of God's gift to us in Jesus. Our praise indeed becomes boundless. The glory he's due indescribable.

So how can we fully express the highest praise this amazing, loving God deserves? Let's consider some creative ways this Christmas to praise and magnify the One who gave his Son to be our Savior. True, we may only have a few days left to incorporate a couple of them this season, but we can save the other ideas for future holiday praise offerings.

To start our list, we'll certainly sing Christmas carols with our church congregations and in our own personal worship times, but we can also join our voices with favorite recording artists as we listen to their holiday music. In fact, let's go beyond humming or casually singing along and genuinely make the message our own. Our praise will soar on wings of joy to the Everlasting Father who orchestrated the coming of the Prince of Peace into a world in desperate need of a Savior. Let's turn these fun sing-along moments into offerings of praise. Into worship.

Other musical praise offerings might include playing an instrument, even something as simple as sleigh bells. Or we could volunteer to rock babies in the NICU and be among the first to softly sing the music of Christmas to them. Or how about caroling in neighborhoods or at a local assisted living facility, a nursing home, or hospital ward? Or teaching our kids or grandkids a carol beloved to us but new to them. We might even try to arrange for a local bell tower to peal the strains of beloved carols at certain times each day. And let's not forget about ringing bells for the Salvation Army during the holiday season. Each of these actions gives us another opportunity for lifting our hearts in praise while perhaps inspiring others to praise God as well.

Artistic expressions of praise to God are not limited to instrumental and vocal music though. We might dance our praise with unbridled joy, or enter a window-painting contest, or help paint a downtown mural or the sets for the church Christmas pageant. We could volunteer our acting talents and play a role in the pageant—or even just attend the performance with a spirit ready to be lifted in praise. Some of us might be able to write a song, a poem, a story, or a play to praise the Lord. Others might offer to help decorate a float for the Christmas parade. Again, all these things done from a heart longing to glorify God become an automatic offering of praise.

Creative praise can also flow from our ordinary speaking voices. Just think of the people we might bless—in addition to blessing God—as we do something as simple as speak. We could offer to read Christmas stories to classes at our local elementary schools or during story hour at the public library. Or we might read Scripture passages pertaining to the birth of Christ to nursing home residents or hospital patients. In fact, they'd enjoy hearing other favorite passages as well.

We could also record Christmas-greeting videos to send to missionaries we know or the ones our church has adopted. We could do the same with our military friends and family members serving overseas and also send a special greeting to their families at home. For long-distance friends and family, we can FaceTime and lift everyone's spirits with "Merry Christmas" wishes and some catch-up conversation. If any have heartaches or special concerns, we could offer to pray with them before ending the call. Some of us may even need to reconcile with someone, and a phone call at Christmas to make things right could be the most important thing we will do this holiday season. What a gift of praise to God—and a gift of love to others—when we use our voices in any of these ways.

Another creative way to praise God during this special season involves the fun of surprise gift-giving. We could spread untold joy by ringing doorbells and leaving surprise gifts for neighbors, friends, and strangers alike. We might even attempt some Secret Santa moves and stay anonymous by disappearing before anyone answers the door. Only the fastest among us will be able to pull that off, but it will create great memories as we give it our best shot. We could also drive through neighborhoods where the homeless camp out and crank up our Christmas music while offering hot chocolate, spiced cider, or steaming hot coffee to those who need a touch of Christmas warmth in more ways than one. I can just imagine the pleasure that this offering of praise would bring to our Lord.

And we mustn't forget one of the simplest ways we can lift our spirits in praise to the Creator of not only Christmas but of the world itself. Spending time outdoors soaking up the sights and sounds of the natural world never fails to point me to the Creator of it all. And as I rejoice in his creation, my spirit worships and praises him at the same time. When we're feeling pressed and stressed during the holiday season—and we certainly will at some point—heading outside for a little nature therapy will set our hearts to praising God in no time at all. We might even be lucky enough to feast our senses on something Christmasy like a new snowfall or the scent of evergreens from fresh-cut wreaths adorning nearby front doors.

As you can see, there's no limit to the boundless ways we can praise God during the holidays. Perhaps these ideas have even triggered others in your mind. Let's throw off restraint and reclaim the beauty and wonder of giving God the glory he's due, the highest praise we can give. After all, he brought hope and salvation to a world lost in sin. He brought them to you. And he brought them to me.

A Song of Christmas Praise

If I could write a Christmas song
It would be a song of praise,
An offering to my God and King
For this holy holiday.

From my heart the words would spring
My spirit would find the tune,
His glory from my lips would spill
Fresh love for him would bloom.

For one joyous night so long ago
My Savior came for me,
To rescue me from sin's dark hold
To give me hope, to set me free.

And now I celebrate his birth
And if I could write a song,
It would be a song of Christmas praise
For to the Savior, I belong!

"He put a new song in my mouth,
a hymn of praise to our God."

Psalm 40:3

Christmas **WISDOM**

We can praise God in countless and creative ways, both during Christmas and beyond.

Christmas **PRAYER**

Lord, with all my heart I'm praising you this Christmas for

Christmas **PAST**

The most creative way I've praised God in past Christmas seasons is

Christmas PRESENT

This Christmas season I will praise God in a new-to-me way by

Christmas MERRYMAKING

Choose at least one of the creative ideas for Christmas praise suggested in this chapter and try it during these remaining days before Christmas. Then on your own or with family or friends, think of some other inventive, out-of-the-box praise ideas you could try either now or in future holiday seasons. Throw off restraint and let the ideas—and the praise—fly!

22

CHRISTMASTIME HOPES

"When Christ was born, so was our hope."[32]

MAX LUCADO

ONCE THE CHRISTMAS TREE GOES up, so do the hopes and dreams of kids everywhere. In a flash, they set their sights on Christmas morning and all the surprises waiting for them then. They count on their every desire to be theirs when that magical day arrives. But kids aren't the only ones brimming with hopes as Christmas approaches. We adults find them springing up in our hearts too. After all, the holidays are naturally a time of hope. A time for wishes to come true.

I've harbored plenty of hopes at Christmastime over the years. I've already mentioned our heart-wrenching hopes as we waited for God to bless our daughters and their husbands with babies. Plus, every Christmas finds me praying for good health and travel weather so our little gang can celebrate together. When grandsons Samuel and Silas had RSV one December, lots of heartfelt pleas sailed heavenward for their recovery in time to join us for Christmas. When God answered our prayers with a "holly jolly" yes, joy overflowed.

And like me, maybe you yearn occasionally for some unforgettable holiday moments to happen. After all, it's the memories made that satisfy the most. So we keep hope alive for special forever memories to carefully tuck away like mementos in a treasure box.

Other hopes may not carry such earnest longing, but they sneak onto our holiday hopes list anyway. Every year I hold my breath and hope my birthday cake for Jesus—the same homemade orange cake my mom made for us as kids on our birthdays—won't be a flop. It can be a tricky undertaking. Fortunately, my family doesn't care what it looks like as long as it tastes good. They accept my cake, imperfections and all, with open arms. Like Jesus, in his mercy, with us.

Another yearly longing of mine ranks much higher in importance than cake. Each fall while pumpkins and mums adorn front porches, a corner of my mind turns to Christmas as I ask God to grace me with an idea and the words for a new poem for my Christmas cards.

The prospect each year of crafting another Christmas poem can feel daunting at the time. Instead of automatically resting in God's faithfulness every year to provide a message wrapped in fine-tuned words, uncertainty niggles instead.

Yes, I am a work in progress. But thankfully, God specializes in using imperfect people to display his glory. He knows my heart. He knows my desire to bless those who read my poems and even point a few lost souls to him in the process. To be part of their journey to faith in Christ.

I hope and pray that those around the world without Jesus will come to know him at Christmas. I pray for missionaries and the open doors the holiday season affords to share the good news of the gospel, to share the hope of Christmas.

Your Christmas hopes may look a little different than mine. Instead of hoping family members can make it home to you for the holidays, you may be hoping to make it home to them. Some of you may be dreaming of a white Christmas so you can enjoy the thrill and beauty of a Christmas-card-perfect holiday. Others may be hoping that nothing will interfere with beloved traditions like attending *The Nutcracker* or participating in a candlelight Christmas Eve service with loved ones.

Some hopes reflect more serious needs and deep desires. Some of you may desperately need a pay raise to ease your financial burdens, while others long to meet someone special or get engaged. Others hope against hope for reconciliation or for physical healing for themselves or a loved one. And some simply long not to be alone this Christmas. Heartache or anguish frames many Christmas hopes, countless Yuletide yearnings.

Let's also consider the hopes surrounding the first Christmas. As soon as God set his grand plan in motion by sending the angel Gabriel to tell Mary the news that rocked her world, the heavenly realm surely rocked with rejoicing and anticipation as well. Every last angel must have wanted to be among those who would fill the night sky and proclaim the Savior's birth. Oh, the joy and thrill of it all—the privilege of bringing such glorious, life-changing news to the world! A Christmas hope, a Christmas dream for them indeed!

And what about Mary and Joseph on that first Christmas night? Once Mary's labor pains began, Joseph's hopes must have immediately fixed on finding lodging in Bethlehem, and perhaps even a midwife who could attend Mary. He undoubtedly hoped and prayed he wouldn't fail in the enormous responsibility God had entrusted to him—being the earthly father, protector, and provider for this Messiah coming as a helpless Babe. This divine One who would be calling him Daddy and depending on him in innumerable ways. Oh, the hopes that must have coursed through Joseph's veins that night!

And Mary? She surely hoped for a comfortable, private place to usher in this extraordinary, God-conceived child of hers. I'm sure she too must have hoped for a midwife while also hoping for the bravery and strength to give birth for the first time.

However, when the stark reality of rustic stable accommodations with no midwife set in, Mary and Joseph's hopes probably shifted solely to the safe delivery of the baby. Here they were, two young people, likely inexperienced in childbirth and parenting, all alone in this new situation fraught with risk. All alone—unless they remembered the God who called them to this task, the God who planted the life within Mary, the God who would surely bring that life into the world by his divine power and protection. Once Mary and Joseph remembered him, peace undoubtedly replaced any panic that threatened.

Once the baby arrived and split the night stillness with his cries, his parents' hopes must have morphed again. As with any new parents, hopes of keeping him safe surely kicked into gear. Plus, the hopes and whispered prayers to successfully fulfill the God-given roles no one before or since would play must have taken on new depth as they held the Messiah, the Son of God, in their arms. Indeed, Mary and Joseph experienced certain hopes and dreams we can only imagine.

With Jesus's birth accomplished, angels were sent and winged their way with divine speed to deliver the grandest birth announcement ever known to man. And with that glorious, angelic proclamation to a few ordinary fellows watching over their sheep in the fields outside Bethlehem, God thrust these lowly shepherds into the middle of the most wondrous story of all time. What hopes might have sprung to their hearts in that moment?

The shepherds first may have only hoped not to be struck dead by this supernatural visitor. But after he announced the most hope-filled, life-giving news of all time—a Savior for all born in Bethlehem that night—their hopes for safety surely rocketed to hopes of finding this newborn Savior for themselves. And off they flew, putting feet to their desire.

Then we have the Magi, probably astrologers but traditionally known to us as the wise men or the three kings of the Orient. Their story, recorded in Matthew 2, tells us after seeing the star of the newborn King, they traveled from far away in the East to come worship him. Their passion to see this new King of the Jews propelled them on their journey. A journey, we can surmise from Scripture, that took up to two years to complete.

The Magi's journey had to be costly and difficult, but they yearned to bow before and worship the new King and present him with gifts of gold, frankincense, and myrrh. When the star they'd been following finally stopped over the house where Jesus was, overflowing joy ensued. Their mission, their dream, had come to pass. They could return home, happy and fulfilled men. And surely changed by their time spent in the presence of the Christ child.

Finally, God must have had hopes of his own on that first Christmas. He must have fervently hoped that the world would joyfully receive this Gift he was sending them. This Savior, his own precious Son, given to redeem all who would accept and worship him. All who would give their hearts to him. High hopes, indeed. Hopes that extend to all people everywhere to this very day.

Yes, Christmas hopes are only natural. They're endless and varied and have been for centuries. But the ultimate

Christmas Hope—the One that stands above all others and will never disappoint—still shines as bright today as his star did in that night sky over two thousand years ago. Jesus, the Hope of the world, our Hope for eternal life, our Hope that will never dim!

The Ultimate Christmas Hope

Christmas is not just a day but a season
A season of joy, peace, and goodwill,
But Christmas also finds us hoping
With hopes we long to see fulfilled.

Some of us hope for good travel weather
So we can spend Christmas with family,
Some hope the gifts we give will please
Some hope to avoid a spending spree.

But some are hoping for deeper things
For their hearts' deepest desires,
Some for a Christmas miracle,
Others for love to transpire.

For many, hope will grow thin
If the miracle slips away,
Their hearts will long for joy and peace
For something to heal the ache.

Thank God for a hope that heals our hearts
The one that is certain and true,
The ultimate Hope born that first Christmas night
The Savior—life eternal—for me and for you.

*"I have come so that they may have life
and have it in abundance."*

John 10:10

Christmas **WISDOM**

Among all the hopes of the season, our hope in Jesus satisfies and comforts like no other.

Christmas **PRAYER**

Lord, you know my deep desire for

Christmas **PAST**

One of the greatest hopes I've seen fulfilled during a past holiday season was when

Christmas PRESENT

Lord, having you as my ultimate hope changes

Christmas MERRYMAKING

Make a list with your family or friends of past Christmas hopes you've seen come true. Tell the stories that go along with them and give God praise for how he blessed. Celebrate with a special dessert or by buying a new Christmas ornament either now or during the after-Christmas sales to commemorate the hopes fulfilled. Or if you'd like to do something super exciting, set off some fireworks. The key word is celebrate!

23

CHRISTMAS JOY

"Good news from heav'n the angels bring,
Glad tidings to the earth they sing:
To us this day a Child is giv'n,
To crown us with the joy of heav'n."[33]

MARTIN LUTHER

WE'RE ON THE CUSP OF Christmas now, aren't we? On the cusp of celebrating the glorious glad tidings first heralded by angels.

As I cock my ear toward heaven and listen back across the centuries to the hours preceding the divine event, I can almost hear the angels calling out to one another, "Did you hear? Mary is in labor!" "She is?! It won't be long now then!" "Surely God will send some of us to proclaim the news when it's time, won't he?" "Oh my goodness, I hope I get to go!" "You can hope all you want. I'm going to get ready!" Yes, they were on the cusp of a joy like no other. Scripture doesn't give us details about what the angels felt at that time, but like I just did, we can certainly imagine what it might have been like.

To fully grasp the joy that flooded the angels, first we must consider the waiting they had to endure. Just think—the waiting began with the prophecies of the coming Messiah, generation upon generation before Mary and Joseph lived the actual story of his birth. Scholars agree that Jesus's birth, life, death, and resurrection fulfilled over three hundred Old Testament prophecies.

Let's reflect on the earliest prophecy for our purposes. As far back as Adam and Eve in the garden of Eden, Scripture records God telling Satan: "And I will put enmity between you and the woman, and between your offspring and hers; he will crush your head, and you will strike his heel" (Gen. 3:15 NIV). The one who crushes Satan's head? Jesus Christ, the Messiah, of course, when he paid for our sins on the cross and rose from the dead, gaining the victory over death, sin, and Satan (Col. 2:9–15). So from humanity's earliest days, the angels awaited the rescue God alluded to in his pronouncement over that scheming Serpent.

We are not told what the angels knew then of God's plan, but we can imagine that as soon as sin entered the world, they knew God well enough to know he would have a plan of rescue for the people he created and so deeply loved. Yes, the angels' expectant wait for the Messiah could easily have started with these very events that Satan's visit to the garden set in motion. And as soon as they began their wait, their joy must have bubbled up, knowing that the great God and King of the universe, the Almighty God they served, had everything in hand. They would one day see him send salvation to the world.

A few prophecies even told of a messenger who would come to prepare the way for the Messiah. The prophets Isaiah and Malachi both foretold of this one who would cry out in the wilderness and prepare the way for the Lord (Isa. 40:3–5; Mal. 3:1). Also, Daniel relays how the angel Gabriel told him about the number of years until the coming of the Anointed One (Dan. 9:20–25). As these pieces of the divine rescue plan came to light, the angels' watchful wait for these events must have taken on a new level of anticipation. The joy that had been simmering in their hearts and minds through the ages must have found fresh freedom to fly a little higher.

Years passed and all of a sudden, the angels' wait grew exponentially shorter. Gabriel had more news to take to earth. And this time it was for the future father of the messenger who would prepare the way for the Savior's coming. I can't be sure, but I suspect Gabriel told some fellow angels about his upcoming mission as he dashed away. Can you just imagine how such news spread like wildfire among the angel ranks as the Father's plan began to unfurl? What jubilance there must have been!

Then at just the right moment—God's ordained moment—Gabriel appeared to the priest Zechariah and told him the most amazing news. Zechariah's barren wife, Elizabeth, whom Scripture described along with him as being well along in years, would bear him a son. And this son, whom they were instructed to name John, would be the long-awaited messenger being sent to prepare the way for the Lord, for the Messiah (see Luke 1:5–24).

From that point on, the waiting periods shifted to shorter time frames. Next up, the angels waited for news of the Savior to be given to Mary and Joseph, the soon-to-be earthly parents of this long-awaited Messiah. Then came the wait through Mary's pregnancy itself. But that had to seem like a flash compared to the hundreds of years the angels had waited before.

Finally, the big day itself came. As I portrayed earlier, I like to think the angels got word of the Messiah's imminent birth as soon as Mary went into labor. Once again, imagine the excitement. The unbridled joy exploding through the heavenlies! What must they have done? What conversations must they have had? Were they similar to the ones I suspected or something completely different? Do you think they hung out near God's throne, hoping to be called on? To be among those who would announce the news to an unsuspecting world?

Once Mary's labor started, the angels' anticipation of being included in the heavenly host that would get to visit the earth had to have swelled to fever pitch. The wait for the Messiah's birth was almost over. With one final exhausted push by his young mother Mary, Jesus—our Hope—entered the world. And with that, the angels rejoiced as never before. Then when God said go, some even had the extraordinary privilege of sharing a peek at heaven's off-the-chart joy with a few lowly shepherds who were watching over their flock in the fields near Bethlehem. Who better to share that glorious celebration with? After all, a little Lamb named Jesus had been born that night, and these faithful shepherds loved and cared for lambs. Oh, the wonder of God's plan—perfect to the tiniest detail.

And today? Even now with each new Christmas celebration, the angels must rejoice as they remember and relive that birth of all births, that night of all nights. Now they lift their heavenly voices with fresh joy, knowing that the Babe who is celebrated is still saving souls today. Still the Savior of the world. Still changing lives and giving hope. Giving a home in heaven and eternal life to all who believe.

That marvelous joy—like that of the angels—can be ours too. That same anticipation, that same unbridled joy. Joy for us at having a Savior. Joy for others because we get to proclaim the good tidings of great joy to them: A Savior for all has been born!

Who can we touch with our Christmas joy this year? Who needs the love and hope of the Savior born for all? May they see the joy and glory of heaven—of Jesus—in us!

Christmas Joy

The long-awaited day had come,
The day the angels had longed for,
The Messiah's birth was to be that night,
Now the world would have its Savior!

Theirs was the job of announcing his birth
And announce it with joy they would,
No greater message could ever be given
No other news could be this good.

What excitement and joy they felt that night
When to some shepherds the news they told,
Their voices rang out like heavenly bells
So glorious, beautiful, and bold.

All around us the angels still praise
This God who gave his Son,
And we need only join their chorus
To feel our Christmas joy begun.

"Suddenly there was a multitude of the heavenly host with the angel, praising God and saying: 'Glory to God in the highest heaven, and peace on earth to people he favors!'"

Luke 2:13–14

Christmas WISDOM

A Christmas joy that's rooted in Jesus will shine like the angels and heaven itself.

Christmas PRAYER

Lord, flood my heart with joy this season that I might ignite it in

Christmas PAST

One of my earliest memories of spreading the joy of Jesus's birth was

Christmas PRESENT

This year my Christmas joy has already splashed over on

Christmas MERRYMAKING

On your own or with family or friends, think of creative ways to allow your joy in a Savior born for all to impact the lives of others. Even though Christmas is almost here, pray for a chance to carry out one or two of your ideas over the next few days and then keep all of them in mind for future holiday seasons.

24

HOME FOR CHRISTMAS

"At Christmas, all roads lead home."[34]

MARJORIE HOLMES

Do you hear it? Can you feel it? Our twirling, whirling world is slowing to a stop so we can all go home for Christmas. So we can gather with our families on these sacred, set-aside days—the very culmination of the season. Yes, Christmas Eve and Christmas Day have arrived.

Of course, the place we consider home changes with the various stages of our lives. During our childhood and young adult years, home revolves around Mom and Dad and our siblings. And when it comes to Christmas, "home for Christmas" simply means being at home with our immediate family and carrying out our beloved must-do traditions. Whether it's a Christmas Eve church service, a reading of "The Night Before Christmas," or opening presents at the crack of Christmas-morning dawn, we're with our closest family members enjoying a warm and homey Christmas. At some point, we may go to Grandma and Grandpa's house, and as we grow older, we realize going there actually feels like "home for Christmas" to our parents. Soon all the grandparent love we experience at Grandma and Grandpa's makes their place a happy extension of home for us as well.

When we marry and have children of our own, we often still go home to Mom and Dad's for Christmas like ours did with theirs, but we also start Christmas traditions with our own little crew. Usually we have to rearrange dates and plans with those in our original family to create a "home for Christmas" experience for our children, but each gathering of loved ones—regardless of when or where it happens—seems to carry that warm, at-home Christmas feeling for all involved.

All too soon and just as surely as the old year gives way to the new, our kids grow up and leave our nest. Before long, they fall in love, marry, and start their own new family units. Such is life. And with it, "home for Christmas" undergoes yet another change.

Whether we're ready for it or not, at that point our home often becomes the extended home. As the grandparents now, we may even be on our own for Christmas Eve or Christmas Day—or both—since we now must share our kids and grandkids with the other side of their family. We experience what our parents did so many years ago. We had no idea how emotional it felt until now.

Through all these "home for Christmas" changes, one thing becomes increasingly clear: That at-home feeling is not confined to one particular place on a certain day. It's the people that are the home. Whenever and wherever our loved ones gather, we've come home for Christmas when we're with them.

Some of you may feel like you don't have a home to go to for Christmas this year—or possibly any year at all now. Maybe you've had a falling out with your family or you live too far away to make the trip home. Maybe you've experienced a deep family loss due to a death or divorce, and the thought of "home for Christmas" brings fresh pain.

Perhaps if you've recently married, you're adjusting to fitting into a new family when you'd rather be with your own. Or maybe you're much older now and roles have changed. You no longer feel central to your family's "home for Christmas" gatherings. You may not be sure where you fit in now. If you feel a bit lost or on the outside looking in as Christmas Eve and Christmas Day arrive, you're not alone.

The year I wrote the poem featured in this chapter, I was struggling with certain aspects of how our lives had changed because of my husband's Alzheimer's. Shortly after Don's retirement, the illness robbed us of our hopes and dreams to move to a community somewhere between where our two daughters and their families lived. A move would not have been good for him, nor would we have the financial freedom to buy the kind of home we were hoping for, not with the future care expenses Don would almost certainly need. The lost dreams cut deep.

In the midst of caregiving, my writing pursuits, and all the other stuff of life that October, I asked God for an idea for that year's Christmas poem, just like I did every year. November arrived in the blink of an eye, and the Christmas-poem clock ticking in my ear added to the pressures I dealt with daily.

During my personal worship time one morning, the uncertainty of where I might live in the future and what decisions I might be forced to make weighed heavy on my heart. As I poured out my concerns and heartache to the Lord about where my home should be, a soul-deep realization dawned crystal clear. With tears in my eyes, I lifted my face heavenward and said, "Jesus, you are my home." Instantly, he whispered to my spirit, "Come home for Christmas." And there it was—my Christmas poem for that year. Oh, what a Savior! Oh, what a Friend! He welcomed me to always come home to him, to always find my peace in him, while also answering my prayer for a poem idea. What peace, what comfort, what joy he gave!

Why not make this priceless comfort and joy your own, my friend? Embrace it. Take it with you. No matter where you are in life or what is happening with your home and family, you will always have a home in Jesus if you've given him your heart. Hear his whisper, hear him say, "Come home for Christmas." This year and every year.

Home for Christmas

This time of year we're all the same
Home is where we want to be,
Even the songs declare it's so,
Home for Christmas is our plea.

Home is where we find the love
Of those who know us best,
The shared traditions, the family bond,
The comfort, the joy, and all the rest.

But there is a home even deeper still
One that won't be shaken, changed, or fail,
It's found in Christ when we believe
An eternal home we'll forever hail.

Yes, Lord, you are my home,
In you I find all, whatever I need,
So when you call, "Come home for Christmas,"
I'll come to you here, there, wherever you lead.

"Jesus answered, 'If anyone loves me, he will keep my word. My Father will love him, and we will come to him and make our home with him.'"

John 14:23

Christmas WISDOM

No matter our family circumstances or current location, if we know Jesus, we can always come home for Christmas.

Christmas PRAYER

Lord, the Christmas longing for home runs deep. Please

Christmas PAST

Having everyone home for Christmas meant the most to me the year that

Christmas PRESENT

This year I'll share a "home for Christmas" feeling with others by

Christmas MERRYMAKING

Make a list on your own or with loved ones of all the different ways Jesus is your home. Turn them into a prayer of thanks. And promise to come home to him wherever he leads—at Christmas and always.

25

CHRISTMAS IS HERE!

"Sing the song of great joy that the angels began,
Sing of glory to God and good-will to man."[35]

JOHN GREENLEAF WHITTIER

CHRISTMAS IS HERE, LET OUR praises ring out! Christmas has come, let's give a shout!

Join me in rejoicing, won't you? Joy to the world!

Jesus our Savior is born!
O come and gaze upon him,
Your Gift, O God, is beyond compare.

To you, God, be glory both now and forevermore!
Our Prince of Peace is with us!

Tell it in the country, tell it in town
Heaven has come to earth,
Evermore hope will reign!

Worship and embrace the Savior as yours
Own the new life he gives,
Rejoice with glorious abandon today
Let others see Jesus in you.
Declare the good news of great joy forever!

THE CHRISTMAS STORY

Luke 2:1–20 KJV

And it came to pass in those days, that there went out a decree from Caesar Augustus that all the world should be taxed.

2 (And this taxing was first made when Cyrenius was governor of Syria.)

3 And all went to be taxed, every one into his own city.

4 And Joseph also went up from Galilee, out of the city of Nazareth, into Judaea, unto the city of David, which is called Bethlehem; (because he was of the house and lineage of David:)

5 To be taxed with Mary his espoused wife, being great with child.

6 And so it was, that, while they were there, the days were accomplished that she should be delivered.

7 And she brought forth her firstborn son, and wrapped him in swaddling clothes, and laid him in a manger; because there was no room for them in the inn.

8 And there were in the same country shepherds abiding in the field, keeping watch over their flock by night.

9 And, lo, the angel of the Lord came upon them, and the glory of the Lord shone round about them: and they were sore afraid.

10 And the angel said unto them, Fear not: for, behold, I
bring you good tidings of great joy, which shall be to all
people.

11 For unto you is born this day in the city of David a
Saviour, which is Christ the Lord.

12 And this shall be a sign unto you; Ye shall find the Babe
wrapped in swaddling clothes, lying in a manger.

13 And suddenly there was with the angel a multitude of the
heavenly host praising God, and saying,

14 Glory to God in the highest, and on earth peace, good
will toward men.

15 And it came to pass, as the angels were gone away from
them into heaven, the shepherds said one to another, Let us
now go even unto Bethlehem, and see this thing which is
come to pass, which the Lord hath made known unto us.

16 And they came with haste, and found Mary, and Joseph,
and the Babe lying in a manger.

17 And when they had seen it, they made known abroad the
saying which was told them concerning this child.

18 And all they that heard it wondered at those things which
were told them by the shepherds.

19 But Mary kept all these things, and pondered them in
her heart.

20 And the shepherds returned, glorifying and praising God
for all the things that they had heard and seen, as it was
told unto them.

Merry Christmas, Friend!
Joy to the World!

ACKNOWLEDGMENTS

I'M SO GRATEFUL FOR EVERYONE who has played a part in this book's journey. Being able to share it with the world is such a gift from God. And it's extra special to me since it includes some of my Christmas poetry—poetry written over forty years of my life.

Heartfelt thanks first to my agent, Karen Neumair, of Credo Communications. No one could have been more supportive and patient as one health crisis after another for either my family or me delayed my work on this project. I'm so grateful that when I was ready, she was ready to help find a publishing home for this book.

My deepest gratitude also to B&H Publishing for seeing this project's potential and saying yes to us. A huge thanks to the entire team—all so gracious and encouraging—who worked with me to help make this book shine. I am beyond blessed to be part of the B&H family now.

My earliest thanks belong to my parents. Mom is already in heaven, but together Mom and Dad fanned the poetic flame in me as they gushed over my first-ever Christmas poem, written for my seventh grade English class. And fifteen years later when I included my next Christmas poem in my Christmas cards, they were the ones who encouraged me to keep the tradition going.

Many thanks also to my Fellowship of Christian Writers group who have not only been great fellow learners, cheerleaders, and prayer warriors, but have become dear friends as well. A special thanks to my critique group who faithfully provided input as the book took shape.

A huge thanks to my ever-faithful prayer team, to my Tuesday morning Bible study group, and to other friends—both in person and online—for all the prayers, encouragement, and friendship you've gifted to me year after year. Everyone needs people like you in their corner.

Special thanks and love to my husband, Don, always the first to read or hear my new Christmas poem each year. With a tear in his eye, he has often said, "That may be your best one yet."

All my love and gratitude also go to my family, both to my own little gang and to the extended group. I am beyond blessed to belong to such a jewel of a family.

An extra shout-out of thanks and love to the live wires in my life otherwise known as my grandsons. After growing up with sisters and having daughters, I've cherished the adventures and memories, the orneriness and fun that comes with being grandma to two sets of twin boys. I hope they know this grandma loves them past the moon and back and always will. I pray this book will be a heritage of faith and family for each of them.

And finally, my eternal gratitude and loving worship to my faithful and loving Lord who has walked with me through all of life. What an incredible privilege he's given me to write words that will point people to him. May we each one be drawn like a magnet to him this Christmas season and beyond.

ABOUT THE AUTHOR

Cheryl Barker has led readers in reflection and encouraged them for years through the written word. She is the author of *Mother of the Bride: Refreshment and Wisdom for the Mother of the Bride* and has written for various other outlets, compilations, and for Blue Mountain Arts greeting cards, gift books, and calendars. Cheryl lives in Kansas and loves to spend time with family, enjoy friends, take photos, and indulge in daily doses of chocolate. She especially loves being grandma to two sets of twin grandsons. Find her online at cherylbarker.net.

NOTES

1. William Spencer, "Be Merry All," *Poems* (London: T. Ca-dell & W. Da-vies, 1811), hymntime.com/tch/htm/b/e/m/e/be_merry.htm.

2. Charles Dickens, *A Christmas Carol* (J. B. Lippincott Co., 1915; Project Gutenberg, 2007, 2019;), 102, https://www.gutenberg.org/cache/epub/24022/pg24022-images.html.

3. Poem by William Cullen Bryant found in *Christmas Memories Keepsake Journal* (Brownlow 2003), hymnary.org/text/as_shadows_cast_by_cloud_and_sun.

4. Joni Eareckson Tada, *A Christmas Longing* (Multnomah 1990, 1996).

5. Pam Brown, *Merry Christmas* (ed. Exley Giftbooks, 1992), lib-quotes.com/pam-brown/quote/lbx7c5k.

6. Evelyn Underhill, *The Letters of Evelyn Underhill* (1936, Charles Williams, ed, book 1943), quotationsbywomen.com/authorq/28796/.

7. *The Letters of Charles Dickens*, vol. 1, 1833–1856 (edited by daughter and sister-in-law) Chapman and Hall, 1880. Note: Letter to Mr. John Forster. 48, Rue de Courcelles, Paris, Sunday Night, Dec. 27th, 1846.

8. John Greenleft Whittier, "Somehow Not Only for Christmas," https://allpoetry.com/poem/14327891-Somehow-not-only-for-Christmas-by-John-Greenleaf-Whittier

9. Christina Rossetti, "In the Bleak Midwinter" (original title "A Christmas Carol"), *The Century Illustrated Monthly Magazine* vol. 3 (1871–1872 Nov-Apr), ed. by J. G. Holland. New York: Scribner & Co: 1872, poetryfoundation.org/poems/53216/in-the-bleak-midwinter.

10. John Francis Wade, "O Come, All Ye Faithful," *The Hymnal for Worship & Celebration* (Word Music, 1986), written 1841, hymnary.org/text/o_come_all_ye_faithful_joyful_and_triump.

11. "The First Noel," *The Hymnal for Worship & Celebration* (Word Music, 1986), written 1833, hymnary.org/text/the_first_nowell_the_angel_did_say.

12. Isaac Watts, "Joy to the World," *The Hymnal for Worship & Celebration* (Word Music, 1986), written 1719, https://hymnary.org/text/joy_to_the_world_the_lord_is_come.

13. "Go, Tell It on the Mountain," Traditional Spiritual first published in *Folk Song of the American Negro* (1907), hymnary.org/text/while_shepherds_kept_their_watching.

14. Watts, "Joy to the World," *The Hymnal for Worship & Celebration.*

15. Henrich Suso, "Good Christian Men, Rejoice," trans. John Mason Neale, 1853.

16. "God Rest Ye Merry, Gentlemen" (16th century England, earliest printed edition 1760, classicfm.com/discover-music/occasions/christmas/god-rest-ye-merry-gentlemen-lyrics-meaning/), www.hymntime.com/tch/htm/g/o/d/r/godrest.htm.

17. Placide Cappeau, "O Holy Night," 1847, trans. John S. Dwight.

18. Quote generally attributed to Bob Hope, appearing in various online sources and articles.

19. Eddie Pola and George Wyle, "It's the Most Wonderful Time of the Year," © Barnaby Music Corp. c/o Songs of Peer, Ltd.

20. "My Study Fire" (ed. 1893), libquotes.com/hamilton-wright-mabie/quote/lbi2i6n. Popular quote online; it is variation of the quote in essay "Christmas," 1863, Quotidiana, ed. Patrick Madden, 9 Sept 2007, http://essays.quotidiana.org/smith_a/christmas/.

21. Mike Dash, "The Story of the World War I Christmas Truce," *smithsonianmag.com*, December 23, 2011, https://www.smithsonianmag.com/history/the-story-of-the-wwi-christmas-truce-11972213/.

22. Mike Case and Sandi Gohn, "For 40 Years, Bob Hope USO Christmas Shows Brightened the Holidays for Deployed Troops," *USO.org*, December 4, 2019, https://www.uso.org/stories/2523-for-40-years-bob-hope-uso-christmas-shows-brightened-the-holidays-for-deployed-troops.

23. Alexander Smith, "A Christmas Carmen," *Christmas Poems* (Barnes & Noble Books, 2002), written 1873, gutenberg.org/files/9574/9574-h/9574-h.htm#link2H_4_0105.

24. John Greenlieaf Whittier, "A Christmas Carmen," *Christmas Poems* (Barnes & Noble Books, 2002), written 1873 gutenberg.org/files/9574/9574-h/9574-h.htm#link2H_4_0105.

25. Phillips Brooks, "O, Little Town of Bethlehem," *The Hymnal for Worship & Celebration* (Word Music, 1986), written 1868, hymnary.org/text/o_little_town_of_bethlehem.

26. William T. Ellis, *Christmas Memories Keepsake Journal* (Brownlow, 2003).

27. Ann Voskamp, *The Greatest Gift: Unwrapping the Full Love Story of Christmas* (Tyndale Momentum, 2013).

28. "God Rest Ye Merry, Gentlemen," www.hymntime.com/tch/htm/g/o/d/r/godrest.htm.

29. worldometers.info/coronavirus/country/us/

30. Joni Eareckson Tada, *A Christmas Longing* (Multnomah Books, 1990, 1996).

31. "The First Noel," *The Hymnal for Worship & Celebration*.

32. Max Lucado, "Christ, Our Hope!" maxlucado.com/christ-our-hope/.

33. Martin Luther, "Good News from Heaven the Angels Bring" (Pennsylvania Lu-ther-an Church Book, 1868), hymntime.com/tch/htm/g/o/o/d/goodnhab.htm.

34. Popular quote online widely attributed to Marjorie Holmes (b. 1910, d. 2002)

35. John Greenlieaf Whittier, "A Christmas Carmen," *Christmas Poems* (Barnes & Noble Books, 2002), written 1873, gutenberg.org/files/9574/9574-h/9574-h.htm#link2H_4_0105.